Leadership in Turbulent Times

A Survival Guide for Leaders in Times of Crisis

Chalondra A. J. Maxwell

Leadership In Turbulent Times

Copyright

Disclaimer

This book is meant for general information and education. The author worked hard for accuracy, but there's no surety it's complete, reliable, current, or error-free.

The author isn't giving professional advice or services. What's here isn't a replacement for talking to pros in that field. The author isn't responsible for what you do based on the info here.

There might be mentions of other sources, websites, or services, but the author doesn't back or guarantee their accuracy, relevance, timeliness, or completeness. The author and publisher don't take responsibility for what those other places say or do. Stories of success or testimonials in this book are about individual experiences. They're not a sure thing for any reader.

Using this book and the info in it is your choice and your risk. You're the one responsible for what you do based on this book, and the author won't be blamed for any harm or losses from using it.

About the Author

Chalondra A. J. Maxwell is a writer, speaker and business personality when it comes to personal

development, finance, and business strategy. Chalondra has devoted her life mission to equipping people with skills that help them achieve financial stability and self-actualization.

The fact that she has done it, indicates how hard she was in pursuit of success. She had a degree in finance and knew the inner dynamics of the financial system. She not only amassed wealth for herself but has improved many people's lives through this knowledge and experience.

Besides the writing, Chalondra A. J. Maxwell is an in demand motivator who addresses different levels of self-actualization speaking on the podiums. This has made her one of the most revered figures in the areas of financial education and personal development because of her magnetic presence on stage and ability to relate with audiences at a deeper level.

Chalondra A. J. Maxwell remains a powerful voice in the sphere of personal development and financial emancipation. These could hold the key to the realization of our success and self-actualization as individuals, societies, countries, regions and the world as a whole.

Table of Contents

CHAPTER 1

CHAPTER 2

Leadership In Turbulent Times

Introduction

Navigating the rough seas calls for more than just common sense; it needs an in-depth change of attitude and perspective. Albert Einstein describes so well in his quote: "The significant problems we face cannot be solved at the same level of thinking we were at when we created them".

Many desire success but only few are ready to walk the rough road from mediocrity towards greatness in this wide world of career dreams. Innately, the majority of people are good; they just need a chance to guide others with honesty and purpose. Nevertheless, the unwillingness to initiate transformational travel from being merely good and becoming great is a sorrowful barrier on the road of success in turbulent times.

The core premise here is clear: The solutions to complicated problems require innovativeness. During volatile periods, leaders must not only deal with crises but also change their ways of thinking in order to effectively manage the new challenges. This evolution of leadership becomes the furnace in which resiliency, flexibility and visionary character are created.

Starting the leadership journey in turbulent times is to acknowledge that past playbooks may be exhausted. The situation has changed, and the regulations have progressed. It requires an admission that the same level of thought that produced existing problems cannot be used as a blueprint for their solution. This runs as the catalytic spark that propels a new age of governance, away from what one is used to into uncharted territory; reacting becomes proactive and good has now become great.

The fact that one cannot ensure the development of the company by maintaining processes and plans in his head has become an alarm bell for action. For menaced scenarios, leadership does not imply a theoretical simulation; it is an ongoing struggle with the current quandaries. Plans must be turned into feasible tactics, and the vision should become steps closer to its concrete realization. It brings attention to the essential feature of hard work—an inexorable pressure towards making dreams come true.

This book sets out on an inward journey into leadership at a time of turbulence, digging deep to understand visionary thinking and emotional intelligence as well as dealing with adaptability that is essential to help organizations navigate stormy waters. Drawing from the words of inspiring leaders and learning to cope with differences that come with transformation, it is about leading not only during periods when things are still under control but also storms in a teacup propelled by negative waves threatening positive focus points at success.

With the pages that follow, we will reveal characteristics to which leadership traits in dynamic times belong—traits beyond common and bring individuals up with organizations on an unprecedented level. This journey begins, and we invite you to accept challenges and learn from provided insights on your way towards leadership involvement in adverse circumstances. These stormy times may weaken us with the test of mettle but they also serve as a platform for great leaders on which to create their own legacy.

Leadership In Turbulent Times

<u>CHAPTER 1</u>

The Leadership In You

Being a leader is more than just being in charge. It is about leading a team to achievements. It's about creating good plans, getting the right communication skills and ensuring that everybody does a task in an efficient manner. Good leaders are inspiring, adjust to problems and respect fairness. They also support the growth of a team, one that helps to guide, learn and develop careers as well as ensuring its success now or in the future.

A leader's goal is to help his or her team make extraordinary achievements. By developing leaders that are capable of building real relationships with workers and maintaining environments elastic for harmony, they ensure the involvement and retention of high-quality performers who thrive in their roles.

Whenever someone is just beginning as a leader or has years upon years of experience under his footing, there will always be some room for improvement. The leaders should continuously develop their skills for them to emerge and become more effective in the roles they play.

Leadership prowess is not necessarily an inherent trait, although a natural inclination towards leadership can promote success. For people who are not born to be leaders, leadership development journey becomes an open-ended process of growth from one level to the next.

This is an overview of these aspects of leadership simplified and outlined in such a way that shows how they all mesh together for making the team successful.

Leadership is not just about issuing orders, it entails making good plans for the future. Leaders should be visionaries and they must base their plans on what the team wants to achieve. They are the architects of a building, designing how everything should fit together to achieve those goals.

Good communicating skills is another necessary component of leadership that makes sure everyone understands plans and ideas, and are on the same page as a team. Good leaders communicate clearly and accept to listen to others. This makes it easier for everyone to work together and creates trust so that they can focus on new ideas.

Leaders should also be motivational. Inspirational leaders should make sure that everyone in the team cares for what they do and does it to their best. Better performance of the entire team occurs when leaders make work feel meaningful and thrilling.

Being a leader also implied the ability to change your approach based on circumstances. Leaders are sometimes forced to take charge and make decisions immediately. Sometimes it's better to work out with the team and allow everyone to have a word. This flexibility helps to cope with different difficulties.

Leadership is not just about the boss; it's also doing the right thing. This enhances trust and gives everyone the assurance that the team is in good hands. Leaders should also consider how their decisions impact others and the world at large.

Helping the team grow is a big part of leadership. Leaders don't just focus on today. They also think about making the team better in the future. This means helping people learn new things, guiding them in their careers, and creating chances for everyone to get better at what they do.

Levels of Leadership

Individual Leadership

Leadership at the individual level is an essential factor for professional success because it ensures personal development and effective team leadership. This approach to leadership states that a person can never lead others unless they learn how to guide themselves. This is significant in terms of the realization that personal development as a leader lays the foundation to one leading on a much larger scale.

Individual leadership, in essence, is like you being the captain of your own vessel – captaining your individual voyage with direction and purpose. This level of leadership is all about the art and knowledge of guiding yourself or self-motivating.

In the vast ocean of life, personal leadership is like a compass that guides individuals through hardships and into opportunities so one can chart out their own path to success. It sheds a light on personal qualities and abilities, acknowledging that before influencing others one must first influence oneself effectively.

Imagine a ship going through choppy waters; the Captain must have an in-depth grasp of his vessel, how far it can go and where he may be heading. Similarly, in the path of life , a person pursuing individual leadership should be self-aware – that is having an intimate knowledge about one's strengths, weaknesses , values and goals.

Self-awareness is the North Star which points to decision making. It enables individuals to act in line with their values, which results in the feeling of genuineness and wholeness. When personal choices sync with core values, people feel meaning and happiness. This alignment forms the basis of personal leadership because it lays a solid foundation upon which one can build his or her life path.

Individual leadership further involves developing a wide range of skills. It's not only about achieving in a specific field but also about acquiring other diverse skills such as the ability to communicate effectively, managing one's time adequately, being adaptable and resilient. These skills are the sails that catch wind of opportunity, sailors toward their dreams.

Individual leadership is very important because it instills in people control over their fates. Instead of being inert passengers, those practicing individual leadership are active pilots who determine the way they want to drive their lives. This feeling of agency is empowering, generating confidence and the belief that one can overcome obstacles.

Good leadership involves effective communication skills. Individual leadership practice requires fine-tuning the skills to communicate ideas effectively, initiate active listening and create favorable communicative surroundings. This mirrors that of a storyteller where leaders present an inspiring tale that is relatable to their team, promoting unity and understanding between members.

Individual leadership is impossible without initiative-taking. Leading others, before leading they themselves have to be proactive and shape their own professional path. This proactive approach is similar to a director writing his or her own career story, making planned decisions and guiding their way toward success. Initiative is the foundation for confident and assertive leadership.

In the world full of changes and uncertainties, individual leadership becomes a reliable anchor. It gives people the mindset and skills to survive storms in order to grab new horizons. Effective individual leadership also involves the capacity to easily adjust oneself in changing circumstances. It's about a strong sailor , who changes the sails when wind changes direction but goes on his travels nevertheless.

There are so many reasons why people embrace individual leadership. Firstly, it gives you a sense of control in an unpredictable world. Life may have unexpected difficulties along the way but a good personal leadership ensures that one is better positioned to sail through these unpredictable waters.

Second, personal leadership encourages proactivity. Instead of reacting to situations, individuals practicing individual leadership are assertive in creating their fates. . This proactive method is empowering and supports a sense of achievement.

Besides, personal leadership matches the natural desire of each human being to develop and grow. It understands that a person is an ongoing project and fosters lifelong learning. With personal leadership, people dedicate themselves to a lifelong quest of self-knowledge and self-actualization that allows them an opportunity for realizing their best.

The lessons learned from self-leadership become a reservoir of knowledge. Every decision taken, every hurdle cleared and success attained adds to a fund of wisdom. This reservoir is not just a static storage but rather an ever dynamic source of wisdom that leaders tap into as they climb the leadership ladder.

Team Leadership

Team leadership is a dynamic and multi-dimensional matrix that connects people who work together to achieve one common major goal. Effective team leadership also requires multiple competencies such as conflict resolution, cooperation within a group and communication. However, the building block of effective team leadership is trust within the group. In this exploration, we discuss the complexities of team leadership in focusing on trust as a key factor that can lead to cooperative behavior and help achieve collective goals.

Managing conflicts that occur naturally within a group is one of the primary challenges faced by team leaders. The skillful conflict resolution is critical to ensure that the team remains harmonious. Leaders will have to provide an environment in which team members do not fear expressing their concerns, and conflicts are seen as opportunities for improvement rather than disturbances. A leader who has mastered the art of mediation is able to transform conflicts into points which can be used as catalysts in innovation and reinforcing better relations among team members.

Innately, team leadership implicates teamwork and thus focuses on the power of individuals when united. A good leader of a successful team is one who knows the strengths and weaknesses of each member in order to create an environment where these characteristics are complemented by our interests.

Promoting teamwork and appreciating the richness of different vision help to develop a stronger, more resilient team. A team leader achieves enhanced coherence in the whole team by implementing a supportive environment where every member feels like an important part of collective effort.

Good and efficient communication is the essence of good team leadership. Leaders should clearly express the team's objectives, demands and achievements to ensure that everybody is on the same page. Also, an excellent team leader is a good listener who values the input and ideas of his members. Regular meetings, updates and feedback ensure inclusivity where team members feel empowered to participate towards the success of a team.

Trust is the foundation of a successful team. Collaboration terminates, innovation stalls if there is no trust in the group. Building and maintaining trust among team members requires investment of time and effort from the leaders. Key elements include consistency, reliability and transparency. Leaders who act with integrity, fulfill their promises and recognize their own flaws inspire trust among the team.

Trust promotes openness in communication where team members feel comfortable to share ideas, give feedback and raise issues without the fear of judgment.

A strong means of instilling trust is by being a role model leader. Team leaders should live by the same values and behaviors that they require from their team. A strong work ethic, a refusal to back down under pressure and steadfast dedication to the goals of one's team are actions that can inspire others. When team members observe their leader is involved in the projects of a team, they are more likely to devote their energy and passion since it creates an atmosphere of common goals where each one competes with another towards the overall objective.

It is crucial for effective team leadership to acknowledge and appreciate team members' contributions. Celebrating successes, big or small, strengthens the positive culture in a team. Recognition creates pride and sense of achievement, inspiring the team members to stay committed in giving their best.

Furthermore, it strengthens the notion that each person's role is significant for the entire team's triumph and fosters a collaborative environment where people support one another.

Organizational Leadership

Organizational leadership is one of the pillars in effective management that frames an entire enterprise to success, by guiding it through strategic thinking and decision-making. It is, at its core, an endeavor in leading a band of people towards common objectives as well as developing harmonious and productive surroundings.

Organizational leadership is very important because it can determine the path of an entire company. This kind of leader should possess a broad knowledge about his or her organization, must understand all the strengths and weaknesses including opportunities for development as well as threats that can undermine successful operations. This wider outlook allows them to articulate strategic initiatives that are rooted in the company's mission and vision.

Strategic mind, a key aspect of organizational leadership is to anticipate the challenges that may arise as well as envision plans for years ahead. Business leaders should also learn to navigate the complicated terrain of business, predicting market tilts and shifts in technology as well competition. By doing so, they would be able to position their organization for sustainable growth and resilience amid uncertainties.

Another important aspect of organizational leadership is decision making, which has to be made quickly and wisely. Sometimes, leaders are faced with situations where they need to balance risks and benefits by considering how the decision will affect different stakeholders. Effective decision making promotes adaptability and makes the organization able to be agile in volatile business climates.

A good organizational leadership is a driving force behind an effective workplace culture. Leaders establish the tone throughout an entire organization and affect employee morale, engagement, and happiness about work. Effective leaders create a culture of support and inclusiveness, which improves teamwork and promotes creativity that fuels innovation, productivity.

Organizational leadership is appealing because it offers a chance to leave an enduring mark. People usually develop leadership positions since they desire to help a bigger body succeed and prosper. The ability to shape the organizational culture, motivate teams and implement transformative strategies is incredibly rewarding.

Furthermore, leadership positions allow for the development and display of one's skills. Leading an entire organization is a challenge that comes with lots of opportunities for personal and professional development. Leadership roles attract individuals with a constant thirst for learning and the opportunity to develop their decision-making skills due to its dynamic nature.

Leadership also enables people to leave a legacy. The successful leaders make their move in the organizations and leave unerasable imprints, leaving tangible strategic initiatives and positive cultural changes behind. This desire to leave behind a lasting legacy is what induces individuals into taking up the obligations and challenges of leading an organization.

Effective communication constitutes a pillar in team building. Organizational leaders are great at defining a vision and making sure that every participant in the team knows where they can contribute to accomplishing common goals. Communication channels that are open and regular allow ideas, feedback, concerns to be circulated with ease in an environment based on trust and transparency.

Organizational leaders focus on the growth and development of their team members. Leaders invest in training, mentorship and professional growth opportunities to empower individuals so that they can fulfill their potential. This personal and professional development commitment nurtures not only people's skills but also fosters loyalty to the organization.

Organizational leadership positions are skilled in identifying and taking advantage of individual abilities within a team. This personalized style of team management equates to assigning tasks that match individual skills, thereby promoting a sense of meaning and achievement. If team members are successful in their roles it will create overall group satisfaction and motivation.

Strategic Leadership

Strategy leadership is about looking beyond the here and now. It's about the building or creating a roadmap that spans into years ahead and what the organization should look like at those points in time. This forward-thinking strategy allows companies to predict challenges and take advantage of opportunities, promoting sustainability and resilience.

Knowledge of the larger environment is like a panoramic view or overall landscape picture. Strategic leaders understand the complexities of an industry landscape, identifying market trends, competitor activity movements and technological changes.

One critical component of strategic leadership is ensuring that every element in an organization supports its broad goals. It's like conducting a symphony, where each instrument plays its part for the perfect harmony. This alignment ensures that all departments teams and individuals are moving in one direction towards the shared vision creating harmony and synergy.

Importantly though strategic leadership isn't a cookie cutter approach. It requires flexibility and keen observation for adjusting sails in accordance with shifting winds. Flexibility is crucial; leaders should be nimble in adjusting strategies as the factors outside change.

This adaptive approach allows organizations to remain relevant and robust amid changing landscapes. Why do people choose strategic leadership? The glamor comes from being able to determine the future of an organization. Strategic leaders are akin to architects, outlining the blueprint of success.

This sense of purpose and influence is a magnetic force, attracting individuals who dream to leave their mark in this world. Furthermore, strategy leadership provides clarity amid ambiguity about the business world. In a world of uncertainties, having a clear vision acts as the North Star for an organization. This clarity informs decision making ensuring employees' confidence in the direction and purpose of the company.

The charm also includes the chance to innovate. The primary task of strategic leaders is to foresee the future and develop innovative solutions that will lead them in its direction. An environment of innovation is attractive to individuals who enjoy pushing boundaries and exploring uncharted territories.

So strategic leaders use many different tested and practical approaches to look into the murky future, trying to forecast trends in order proactively plan.

These practices collectively form an effective toolkit that allows organizations to deal with uncertainties and capitalize on the opportunities presented by events in the future.

An in-depth environmental analysis is one of the cornerstones of predicting the future. Strategic leaders go about conducting thorough environmental scanning of their external environment paying close attention to market trends, economic indicators and geopolitical changes. This constant review acts as a kind of radar system that leaders use to detect early signs of change, and adapt their strategies.

Leaders must be aware of the surrounding environment at all times so that they can identify unrealized opportunities or potential issues before these become more significant and obvious.

Scenario planning is yet another potent weapon in the arsenal of strategic leaders. Instead of taking a single forecast to plan ahead, scenario planning implies the creation of multiple future scenarios based on different premises. This method enables leaders to prepare for different potential situations, encouraging flexibility and adaptability. It's like having a set of contingency plans in place for the organization to be able to pivot fast enough in response to any changing circumstances.

Data analytics are also manipulated by strategic leaders. In the information age, mounds of data are created every day. This data enables a valuable analysis of the consumers and market patterns, as well as emerging trends. Through data analytics, leaders can make educated decisions about anticipating future patterns and perfect their strategies to achieve the best results.

Foresight tools including trend analysis and predictive modeling are like the crystal balls of strategic leaders. Trend analysis refers to the study of historical patterns in order to identify recurring themes and possible trends. Predictive modeling uses mathematical equations to predict future progress using current information. These tools increase a leader's effectiveness at making predictions based on data, helping develop strategies that conform to current trends.

It is valuable to establish strategic partnerships not only for the present but also foreseeing future collaborations. Strategic leaders identify potential collaboration opportunities that fit their long-term perspective. All these alliances can provide access to new markets, technologies or complementary strengths. By partnering with those who hold similar views, leaders build a network that increases their collective power to adapt in an environment which is constantly changing.

Strategic leadership is characterized by the proclivity to embrace innovation. Leaders promote an environment of innovation and learning within their organizations. By creating a culture in which new ideas are encouraged and failure is considered the path to success, leaders make sure that their teams' boundaries keep on being pushed farther and farther apart. This innovation approach puts the organization ahead of its competition.

The other area of foresight is customer feedback and insights. Strategic leaders do not fail to appreciate their customers' needs and preferences. Continuous asking for feedback, surveys and close observation of customer behaviors offer priceless ammunition in predicting market changes. By paying close attention to customer sentiments, leaders can develop their strategies in line with changing expectations.

Strategic leaders also use talent management and development as a way of future-proofing their organizations. First of all, recognizing the value that workforce has as a main success driver, leaders cultivate teams with various skills and perspectives.

Transformational Leadership

Transformational leadership is an approach even more potent than mere management because it involves inspiring people, motivating them and making real changes in the course of a company or organization. At the core of this leadership style, we see such leaders as those who not only lead their teammates but also manage to create inside them a kindling for achieving great heights.

It is the inspiration and motivation that are at core of transformational leadership. Transformational leaders do not rely only on their authority to gain the respect of those they lead, but help them develop a sense of shared vision and common purpose. They vividly depict an alluring future that unites team members into a shared vision, which is beyond the scope of separate chores.

This makes people excited and committed, helping to establish a workplace where the individuals are not simply taking orders but actively pursuing some higher purpose.

One critical characteristic of a transformational leader is being able to cultivate confidence and faith in the team's abilities. ···leaders using this style often show absolute confidence in their team members, encouraging them to step out of their comfort zones and strive for bigger goals. This is an affirmation that increases the self-esteem of individuals as well collectively which has a beneficent circularity where greater confidence enhances performance and so on.

Transformational leadership is characterized by organizational change. Change agents are leaders in this category who are not satisfied with the status quo. They realize the need to change their approach when circumstances keep changing and steer teams through such transitions.

Transformational leaders are also at the helm, driving leadership toward innovation and growth – whether it's embracing new technologies, reshaping processes or even rewriting a company's mission.

The value of transformational leadership becomes clear because it can create a culture for continuous improvement. Leaders advance creativity and free dialogue to inspire their teams not only beyond ordinary tasks but also innovative solutions. This does not only improve problem-solving but also provides an atmosphere in which employees feel appreciated for their contribution, increasing job satisfaction and loyalty.

Transformational leadership attracts people for various reasons. First, it creates a sense of purpose and meaning in the workplace. When workers feel that they are contributing to a bigger purpose in their work this makes them have more job satisfaction and overall happiness. Secondly, emphasis on individual growth attracts workers who are interested in personal and professional improvement. Transformational leaders provide mentorship and support, which helps team members develop more skills and enhance their capabilities.

Additionally, the collaborative character of transformational leadership makes for an intense atmosphere of teamwork. The focus on collective goals and mutual support is a unified work environment in which people feel that they belong to something special, like family. This sense of unity smoothes daily operations and largely contributes to the overall success of an organization in the long run.

Servant Leadership

It is an enchanting philosophy of leadership that clearly emphasizes on the element of servitude and supporting team members with total devotion to their well being. Fundamentally, a servant leader turns the concept of leadership on its ear and places themselves as overseers for their team's success in place of bosses.

Servant leadership is based on the principle of commitment to serving others selflessly. This means that the leaders should be proactive in finding chances to help their team members and create a

40

conducive environment where every individual can succeed. This is because this approach looks beyond the professional development of an individual to also ensure that their personal needs and concerns are adequately addressed.

By putting the welfare of team members first, servant leaders promote a culture grounded in empathy, trust and cooperation.

Empowerment is one critical component of servant leadership. Servant leaders identify the unique potential that each member of their team has, and they endeavor to unlock this by offering them direction, support in terms of resources and motivation. They do not micromanage but rather place their trust in the team to succeed, fostering a sense of ownership and freedom. It creates a sense of empowerment which is good not only on an individual level but also when it comes to team success.

Importantly, servant leadership is a proactive and all-embracing philosophy. Leaders are good listeners to their team, appreciating different views and creating an environment of inclusion. This all encompassing attitude lends an air of belonging which enhances morale and motivation among team members. This, in turn, has a positive impact on productivity and innovation within the team.

Why is servant leadership important? In a fast-changing professional environment that can be quite complicated and dynamic, this leadership style is shown to be an effective and flexible model. By focusing on the well-being of team members, servant leaders create strong and united teams capable of navigating a variety of challenges successfully. This not only ensures the success of the team in recent times but also lays a solid basis for ongoing growth.

Servant leadership attracts people for different reasons. First of all, it is consistent with universal human values such as compassion and altruism. Human beings by nature tend to respond positively when they feel that they are genuinely cared for and supported. Servant leadership cultivates this basic need for connection and fosters a workplace culture that recognizes people not just as task performers but also as individuals with dreams and problems.

Secondly, servant leadership encourages a sense of purpose. An emotional connection results in positive feedback as team players are encouraged to return with the support that they receive and this eventually leads on towards a cooperative style of work.

Although servant leadership presents commendable benefits, it is essential to note its drawbacks and possible pitfalls.
One significant weakness in servant leadership is the possibility of ambiguity whilst making a decision. This focus on cooperation and consensus-building may result in the delay of decision implementation.

In circumstances where quick and decisive actions are needed, the inclusiveness that comes with servant leadership might slow down decision making. Considering the opinions and well-being of all team members could lead to loss of precious time in urgent situations.

Servant leadership may not be effective in circumstances where hierarchical structures and defined authority are crucial. In some industries or situations, a more directive style is needed for organizational effectiveness. Servant leaders have difficulty gives clear direction and assertive decision-making when the team resist or be ambiguous,

There is also another possibility of leaders overlooking their own needs. Though in the servant leadership model, they pay more attention to the well-being of their team members yet there is a risk that leaders can neglect their own development whether it's professional or personal.

An imbalance of this nature may gradually cause burnout and make an individual less effective over time. It is important for leaders to strike a fine balance between serving others and ensuring their own growth and sustainability in the role of leadership.

In addition, servant leadership could be difficult to practice in settings where performance metrics and tangible results are of utmost importance. In environments where outcomes are carefully examined, the focus on nurturing individual growth and well-being may be perceived as not putting enough emphasis on achieving measurable goals. This may generate skepticism or resistance from stakeholders who focus on tangible outcomes over the less measurable elements of leadership.

Charismatic Leadership

Charismatic leadership is an impressive style of interaction, where people use their charisma and sense to convince others. In other words, it is the science of winning hearts and minds with a persuasive personality. This style of leading surpasses conventional authority — based not on positional power but personal magnetism.

The charismatic type of leaders are those who possess a certain allure that attracts people to them. Think of a leader who is confident, communicates enthusiastically and cares for people – these three characteristics are what defines charismatic leadership.

One of the critical aspects of charismatic leadership is that such a leader can inspire absolute loyalty and devotion among followers. Charismatic leaders are able to convey a powerful vision, one that inspires the ambitions and ideals of their believing audience.

In addition, charismatic leadership has a transformational effect on organizational culture. Charismatic leaders bring infectious enthusiasm to help create a positive and energetic work environment. Team members are not just carrying out tasks; instead, they all play an integral part in a common vision. That collective sense of purpose boosts morale, encourages teamwork and provides a common cause towards succeeding.

Also, charismatic leaders are good at developing a profound feeling of trust. Their authentic connections to their team in combination with transparency creates a trust framework that is integral for productive collaboration. Such trust fostered by charismatic leaders becomes an engine of unity and productivity in times when skepticism towards authority will get deeper.

For many reasons, people are attracted to charismatic leaders. First of all, the human mindset is set up to react favorably towards charisma. The charisma of a leader cultivates certain psychological magnetism that attracts focus and inspires people to admire it. This natural attraction goes deep into our evolutionary past where powerful, charismatic individuals often were instrumental to the survival of whatever population group they are put in.

More importantly, charismatic leaders tend to be self confident even in difficult times. In unclear and ever changing situations, people seek for leaders who can rise above complexity with ease. The charismatic nature of a leader offers an assurance, creating confidence and faith in the collective strength to surmount all challenges.

Charismatic leaders have this incredible way of connecting with people emotionally. They really understand the feelings and needs of their team, making it more than just a job and turning it into a meaningful journey.

What makes them stand out is their emotional intelligence – they can read and respond to emotions effectively, creating deeper connections. They also have this visionary quality, where they can paint a clear and inspiring picture of the future for the organization. This helps guide the team with a sense of purpose beyond the daily challenges.

Charismatic leaders are also super creative thinkers. They approach problems with an open mind, coming up with innovative solutions. This kind of thinking is crucial in careers where things are always changing.

Their ability to communicate ideas persuasively is another strength. They can motivate others and get them on board with their vision through effective communication, creating a shared belief in common goals.

Strategic thinking is a big part of their game too. They're excellent at planning for the long term, understanding organizational goals and making sure their vision turns into real results. And they're always learning – these leaders have a constant thirst for knowledge, setting an example for curiosity and growth in their teams.

Adaptive Leadership

Leading adaptively is like being the captain of a ship in a stormy sea, navigating through rough waters by adjusting sails with changing winds. In our ever-changing world, where change and uncertainty are always around, adaptive leadership becomes a crucial guide for steering organizations through transformation.

Think of a traditional leader as someone following a set route on a map, regardless of unexpected obstacles. Adaptive leaders are like explorers with compasses, acknowledging that the landscape can change. They adjust to the terrain instead of stubbornly sticking to a predetermined path.

Flexibility is key for adaptive leaders. They bend and flex, absorbing shocks and understanding that plans might need tweaking. When faced with unexpected turns, they pivot gracefully, finding new ways forward.

Learning and adaptability are a dynamic duo for adaptive leaders. They continuously learn from experiences, refine strategies, and reshape their approach to match the ever-changing landscape.

Adaptive leadership is like a sought-after treasure because, in a world where change is constant, organizations need leaders who can navigate uncertainty, not just go with the flow. Traditional leadership can find itself sailing in outdated waters. Adaptive leaders inspire trust by being honest about not having all the answers. They admit that the seas ahead might be uncharted, building a secure crew that knows their captain is steering with agility.

Moreover, adaptive leadership sparks innovation. Like a gardener tending to a diverse garden, adaptive leaders nurture an environment where different ideas bloom, encouraging creative thinking.
Adaptive leadership is a survival skill in the fast-paced jungle of change. Organizations choose it because it's about embracing the unknown, staying relevant, responsive, and resilient.

However, challenges and drawbacks exist. Resistance to change is a formidable adversary. Human nature resists the unfamiliar, and constant adaptation may face pushback within the team, challenging resilience.

Decision-making becomes a complex puzzle. Unlike traditional leadership with a fixed playbook, adaptive leaders face intricacies. The absence of a fixed roadmap means decisions must be made amid uncertainty, slowing down the process.

Balancing stability and change becomes a delicate act. Too much change too quickly can lead to chaos, while too little may result in stagnation. Striking the right balance demands astute leadership and a nuanced understanding of the organization.

Communication is crucial. Frequent shifts in direction demand clear and transparent communication. Leaders must articulate the rationale behind changes to ensure the team understands and remains aligned with organizational goals.

Yet, challenges extend beyond interpersonal dynamics. The risk of burnout looms large. The perpetual need for adaptation can lead to fatigue among leaders and team members, jeopardizing sustained performance.

The lack of a clear roadmap adds complexity. Adaptive leadership might lack a clear roadmap due to its fluid nature. This ambiguity can be disconcerting for those who prefer structured guidelines, posing a challenge in managing expectations.

In the pursuit of immediate challenges, adaptive leaders might overlook long-term goals. Focusing too much on short-term adaptability could result in neglecting strategic planning and the cultivation of a vision for sustained success.

Resistance from entrenched organizational structures poses a hurdle. Hierarchical organizations with rigid structures may resist the paradigm shift in adaptive leadership, necessitating a careful recalibration of the organizational mindset. Skill and competency gaps can impede successful implementation. This leadership style demands a specific set of skills, including emotional intelligence, quick learning, and strategic thinking, posing challenges for leaders who may not possess these skills.

CHAPTER 2

The Man Who Thought Differently

American creator, designer and businessperson Steve Jobs is an important figure in establishing and leading Apple Inc. He was born in 1955 to grad students studying at the University of Wisconsin who adopted him out. He quit college, tried different things and in 1976 found partner with Steve Wozniak to form Apple.

Jobs departed from Apple in 1985 but returned over a decade later. His contribution to modern tech is enormous, developing revolutionary gadgets such as iPhone, iPad and iPod that influenced the world of technology. In 2011, unfortunately Jobs fought pancreatic cancer until he died.

Jobs grew up in Mountain View, California which later became part of Silicon Valley and his curiosity led to some accidents. As a toddler, he took himself twice into the emergency room – one time for poking in an electrical socket with a pin and second for swallowing poison.

– At first working in the family garage with his dad on electronics, Jobs learned to take things apart and then reassemble them, gaining confidence as well as mechanical skills. He was well-educated, but formal schooling irritated him and the tricks played by him at his elementary school were a result of his boredom.

In high school at Homestead, Jobs joined the Explorer's Club in Hewlett-Packard where he met computers for the first time. He got a summer job in HP where Steve Wozniak, his future partner of Apple was introduced.

Jobs went to Reed College in Portland, Oregon but only stayed for six months after high school. In the following year and half he dabbled into creative classes. A calligraphy class ignited his passion for typography.

In 1974, Jobs was a video game designer at Atari but only stayed for a couple of months before heading to India in search of spiritual enlightenment. His life involved drugging with mind-altering substances, punctuating an era of exploration and self knowledge.

1974 was the short period in which Jobs worked as a video game designer at Atari, another big name associated with the early history of video games. He worked for Atari for a short time where he helped develop video games but left soon after to search for the inner enlightenment in India. In the early days of video gaming, Atari played a critical role that influenced development in creating iconic games and consoles for this market.

Founding and Leaving Apple Computer Inc.

1976 was the year when Jobs had just turned 21 and together with Wozniak, co-published Apple Computer Inc. from within Jobs' family garage. Jobs sold his Volkswagen bus, and Wozniak his favorite scientific calculator to finance their venture. These are the guys through whom Apple is credited with revolutionizing personal computers. They made them smaller, cheaper and intuitive for regular people to operate them easily.

Wozniak put together some user-friendly personal computers and with Jobs doing their marketing, Apple first sold these computers at $666.66. They earned approximately $774,000 with the Apple I. Sales then took off three years after the second model, Apple II, skyrocketing to $ 139 million.

1980 saw Apple Computer going public; and by the end of its first day, it had a worth $1.2 billion. But then, Apple stumbled with some flawed products, recalls and ultimately upset customers. By then, IBM took over in sales while Apple had to meet an IBM PC-oriented business arena.

In 1983, Apple hired marketing whiz John Sculley of Pepsi-Cola as CEO brought in by Jobs. The next year, they released the Macintosh, marketing it as part of a counterculture lifestyle: romantic, youthful, and creative. Although the Macintosh sold well and had better specifications than IBM's PC, it was not an IBM-compatible product.

Sculley believed that Jobs was a troublemaker, and those in charge of Apple were forcing him further away. In 1985, Jobs left the company he co founded without an official title.

In 1985, after leaving Apple Inc, Jobs invested $12 million into NeXT Inc, which was a hardware and software venture company. In 1988 they released their first computer targeting universities and researchers, but the price of $6,500 was out of reach for many people.

The company's operating system, NeXTSTEP, performed better and was used by programmers to develop games such as Quake and Doom. The first web browser designer was Tim Berners-Lee, and he used a NeXT computer. NeXT could not reach mainstream America, and in 1996 Apple purchased the company for $429 million.

In 1986, Jobs acquired an animation company owned by George Lucas that later turned into Pixar Animation Studios. Jobs invested $ 50 million of his own money when he believed in Pixar's potential.

The studio went on to make really loved movies like Toy Story (1995), Finding Nemo (2003), The Incredibles (2004), Cars (2006), and Up (2009). In 2006, Pixar joined forces with Disney, and that made Jobs the biggest shareholder of Disney.

Returning to and Reinventing Apple

In 1997, Jobs returned to Apple's position as CEO, and yet again he is lauded for resurrecting Apple during the 1970s. Jobs changed Apple into a company with new management crew, adjusted stock options and an annual salary of just $ 1. His intelligent products such as the iMac, smart marketing and stylish designs made Apple popular again.

Apple introduced groundbreaking products such as the MacBook Air, iPod and iPhone in subsequent years that shaped the tech world. When Apple introduced something new, competitors were quick to follow suit. In 2007, to coincide with its broadened range of products, the company renamed itself Apple Inc.

Apple's quarterly reports in that year were impressive: Stocks reached $199.99 a share, the company earned an astonishing profit of $1.58 billion, had cash reserves and no debt at all.

By 2008, thanks to iTunes and IPods, Apple was the second largest music seller in the U.S., behind only Walmart. Apple also secured the number one position on America's Most Admired Companies and Fortune 500 for shareholder returns.

Since the launch of the iPhone in 2007, Apple has produced various iterations. In February 2023, a used iPhone reached above $63 thousand in an auction.

Forbes states that before his death in 2011, Jobs' net worth jumped to $8.3 billion. Celebrity Net Worth has even estimated it was as high as $10.2 billion .

Apple reached a $3 trillion market cap in January 2022, Jobs' startup stake from the beginning of his career in 1980 would have put him at nearly $330 billion – enough wealth that he'd eclipse even Elon Musk if still alive. But, according to the New York Post , in 1985 Jobs sold off nearly all his Apple shares.

Most of Jobs' wealth came from an 8 percent share in Disney he got when he sold Pixar in 2006. Based on Disney's 2022 value, that share, now with his wife, is worth $22 billion.

2003 saw Jobs diagnosed with a rare though curable form of pancreatic cancer known as neuroendocrine tumor. Instead of quickly jumping into surgery, he decided to modify his pesco-vegetarian diet and investigate Eastern approaches. Jobs delayed the surgery for nine months, and Apple's board members were uneasy. Execs feared that if news of the CEO's illness got out, shareholders might run away. Jobs eventually gave more importance to his privacy than exposing the reality of health status before shareholders.

2004 was the year in which Jobs successfully underwent a surgery to remove his pancreatic tumor. As usual, he remained low-key regarding his health during the subsequent years.

Early 2009 saw rumors about Jobs' weight loss on the rise with talk that he was ill again, perhaps even receiving a liver transplant. Jobs explained, citing a hormonal imbalance and soon after took a leave for six months.

In an employee memo, Jobs revealed that his health issues were more complicated than he first imagined and made Tim Cook responsible for running Apple on a day-to-day basis.
Jobs came back almost a year later in September 2009, to debut the iPad at an invitation-only Apple event. In 2010 he remained in the lead.

By January 2011, Jobs again announced another medical leave. In August, he resigned from Apple CEO and handed it over to Cook. He officially died of respiratory arrest due to his long struggle against pancreatic cancer.

Left in his last weeks, Jobs, who was weak, struggled to climb stairs but still succeeded to see off colleagues like Disney CEO Bob Iger, even meet with the author of biography and advised Apple executives on iPhone 4S launch. In a eulogy, sister Mona Simpson shared that, just before his passing, Jobs gazed at his sister, Patty, then his wife and kids, looked beyond them, and uttered his final words: "Oh wow. Oh wow. Oh wow."

His Leadership Role can Play an Integral Part in Shaping our Perspective on Leadership

In 1976, Steve Jobs began Apple in his parents' garage and that led him to hit rock bottom, but he later brought the company back from seemingly facing bankruptcy. Through his efforts, by the time he died on October 5, 2011. And henceforth it had become the most valuable company on earth.

Throughout his journey, he transformed seven industries: 3D technology has been applied to a number of fields such as personal computing, animated movies, music, phones, tablet computers, retail stores and in digital publishing. Consider him on par with America's greatest inventors such as Thomas Edison, Henry Ford and Walt Disney. They were not saints, and history will depict how imagination merged with technology and business.

Jobs' personality was a big part of how he did business. He acted like the usual rules didn't apply to him, pouring passion, intensity, and extreme emotions into both his everyday life and the products he created. His impatience and perfectionism went hand in hand.

He once said, "Look at the results. These are all smart people I work with, and any of them could get a top job elsewhere if they felt truly beat down. But they don't. And we got some amazing things done."

Over the past dozen years, Jobs and Apple achieved a string of hits greater than any other innovative company in modern times. iMac, iPod, iPod nano, iTunes Store, Apple Stores, MacBook, iPhone, iPad, App Store, OS X Lion—not to mention every Pixar film. Battling his final illness, Jobs was surrounded by an intensely loyal group of colleagues and a loving family.

The real lessons from Steve Jobs, I believe, come from examining what he actually accomplished. Creating a lasting company, he said, was harder and more crucial than making a great product. How did he pull it off? Business schools will be studying that question for years to come. Here are what I see as the keys to his success.

Focus

When Steve Jobs came back to Apple in 1997, things were all over the place – too many computers, peripherals, Macintosh versions. One day, he had enough. "Hold up!" he yelled. Grabbed a marker, strolled barefoot to a whiteboard, drew a simple grid: "Consumer" and "Pro" on top, "Desktop" and "Portable" on the side. He said, "Let's focus on four great products, one for each box. Cancel everything else."

There was silence among his team members but, by narrowing down to four computers, he saved Apple.

"Deciding what not to do is as crucial as deciding what to do," he'd said.

Later on, Jobs took his top team on an annual retreat. On the last day, he stood by a whiteboard (he loved those) and asked, "What should we do next?" His team pitched ideas, he wrote them down, and then he'd scratched off what he thought was dumb. After some back and forth, they'd settled on 10 things. But Jobs wasn't done – he'd slashed seven and said, "We can only do three."

Focus was Jobs's thing, shaped by his Zen training. He filtered out distractions, even if it frustrated colleagues and family. Near the end of his life, he advised Larry Page, the guy taking over Google. Despite their companies feuding, Jobs shared wisdom. "Focus," he emphasized. Told Page to figure out what Google wants to be when it grows up. "Narrow it down. Get rid of the extras dragging you down. Don't be like Microsoft. Aim for greatness, not just adequacy." Page took the advice, focused on a few key things in 2012, echoing Jobs's approach.

If you want things to be clearer, have more energy, and see way better results, you'll find these ideas super helpful. it's all about getting the most out of your focus. Start with something rarely mentioned but super important. To seriously boost your success, put all your focus into just a few projects.

Why focus on less projects? In your role as a small business owner or consultant, allocating your focus to a select few projects is crucial due to limited resources. By concentrating on one idea at a time, you enhance effectiveness and eliminate Mind Fog associated with juggling multiple tasks.
This also clears out mind fog – that fuzzy thinking from focusing on too much at once.

Steve Jobs talked about focus at a conference in 1997. He said focus is not just saying yes to what you're working on; it's saying no to many other good ideas, you need to pick carefully. He was proud of the things Apple said no to – innovation is about saying no to many things.

The lesson is clear. figure out the best use of your focus in your plans, then, give that project or idea all your time. Still not sure? you've seen this in action when someone talks passionately about a project. High-energy entrepreneurs focus sharply, bring clarity, increase direction and purpose, and then they're all set to go!

Simplify

Jobs had this amazing ability to really focus on the heart of things, making things simple by getting rid of anything unnecessary. Apple's first brochure said, "Simplicity is the ultimate sophistication," and you see it when you compare Apple software to, let's say, Microsoft Word – Apple keeps it clean, while Word gets messier.

His love for simplicity started back when he worked the night shift at Atari. Their games had to be simple enough for anyone, even a stoned college freshman, to figure out. This idea of simplicity stuck with him, especially after attending design conferences that emphasized clean and functional design.

When Jobs saw plans for a computer with a graphical user interface and a mouse at Xerox, he made it even more user-friendly and simpler. He wanted a mouse with one button that cost $15, not three buttons like the Xerox one that cost $300. Jobs aimed for a kind of simplicity that comes from conquering complexity, not just ignoring it.

In Jony Ive, Apple's designer, Jobs found someone who shared his passion for deep simplicity. They knew it wasn't just about having a minimal look, but about understanding every part deeply. Ive said, "To be truly simple, you have to go really deep."

Even in designing the iPod interface, Jobs pushed to cut out unnecessary stuff. He insisted on getting to whatever you wanted in just three clicks. Once, he suggested getting rid of the on/off button, and the team realized it wasn't needed. The device could power down on its own and wake up when needed.

Jobs always looked for industries making things more complicated than needed. In 2001, it was music players and buying songs online. Then came mobile phones, where he pointed out how confusing they were. Towards the end, he was eyeing the television industry, wanting to simplify how people watch what they want.

Steve Jobs' impact on the tech world came from keeping it simple. From iPhones to Macs, he led Apple with a focus on simplicity. The iPod, a game-changer, ditched complexity for sleek, modern simplicity. Leaders and entrepreneurs, take note. Don't complicate; stay focused like Jobs did, akin to his straightforward wardrobe.

Jobs showed that simplicity wins. Smartphones and computers under his guidance thrived due to their easy design. The iPod's revolution laid in shedding excess, embracing a smooth, modern, and, above all, simple approach.

What's the lesson for leaders? Avoid overcomplicating. Stick to the essentials. Just as Jobs curated simplicity in electronics, leaders should streamline their strategies. Imagine his wardrobe – no fuss, just the essentials.

Why did Apple soar? Jobs understood the allure of simplicity. In a world drowning in complexities, his products stood out. Entrepreneurs, take heed. The key is not to overwhelm but to simplify. Jobs' success mantra was clear: focus and simplicity.

Consider the iPod. It wasn't a maze of features. Instead, it offered simplicity in a sleek package. Leaders, apply this philosophy. Cut the noise. Like Jobs' iconic turtleneck, keep it simple, yet impactful.

So, for leaders and entrepreneurs embarking on ventures, remember Jobs' legacy. Don't let complexity cloud your vision. Jobs' triumphs were in uncomplicating the tech industry. Your path to success? Embrace simplicity, maintain focus, and let your strategy mirror Jobs' minimalist wardrobe.

Assume Full Responsibility from Start to Finish

Steve Jobs was onto something big when he insisted on the Apple way – making sure hardware, software, and extras all move together seamlessly. Take the iPod and Mac marriage through iTunes. This magic move simplifies devices, smoothens syncing, and tames glitches. Jobs wasn't just solely interested in selling gadgets. He wanted an Apple ecosystem where everything just clicked.

Jobs wasn't a fan of the scattergun approach other companies took. He and Apple owned the user experience from start to finish. From the iPhone's microprocessor to snagging one at an Apple Store, Jobs tied every customer touchpoint into a neat bow. Microsoft and Google went with an open-door policy, letting any hardware maker use their software. Jobs wasn't buying it. For him, it was a shortcut to "crappier products." His logic? People are busy; they don't want to wrestle with tech. They just want it to work.

Jobs's quest for perfection meant he had to be the puppet master, pulling the strings of "the whole widget." Sure, he had a control freak streak, but it wasn't just about feeding his ego. He couldn't stomach the idea of his perfect Apple world being tainted by unapproved apps or content. It wasn't always the quickest route to profit, but in a world drowning in subpar gadgets and confusing interfaces, it birthed stunning products.

So, what's the message for leaders and entrepreneurs? Take charge. Be the captain of your ship. Jobs didn't just oversee a product; he curated an experience. He took responsibility for every hiccup and triumph from the microprocessor to the store shelf. It's tempting to go the Microsoft or Google way, flinging your software open to anyone with a chip. But Jobs thought that led to a chaotic garden, not a Zen one.

Jobs didn't want you wondering if your hardware could keep up with Apple's genius software. He wanted you gliding through an experience so smooth it felt like walking through a Japanese garden.

Now, the open-door approach has its perks. More players, more options, maybe more profit. But Jobs cared about the endgame, not just the scoreboard. He didn't want a forest of gadgets; he wanted a curated garden. So, leaders, entrepreneurs, take a moment. Reflect on Jobs's journey. It is not always an easy path. It was the one that led to Apple becoming a flourishing company.

Stay Hungry, Stay Foolish

Steve Jobs got influenced by two big things in the late '60s in the San Francisco Bay Area. First, there were the hippies and antiwar folks who were into things like trippy drugs, rock music, and not liking people in charge. The second thing was the tech and hacker scene in Silicon Valley, where you had lots of brainy people like engineers, geeks, and entrepreneurs doing their thing in garages.

Both paths to personal enlightenment, like Zen and Hinduism, meditation, yoga, and other philosophies, influenced Jobs.

Publications like Stewart Brand's Whole Earth Catalog, which focused on "access to tools," captured the mix of these cultures. Jobs, who embodied a mix of hippie, rebel, spiritual seeker, phone phreaker, and electronic hobbyist, was a fan. He was especially taken by the last issue's message, "Stay Hungry. Stay Foolish."

Throughout his career, Jobs kept a blend of his business and engineering side with the nonconformist, hippie rebel from his earlier days. Even as Apple became more corporate, he injected a rebel spirit into its ads. The famous "1984" ad portrayed a renegade woman challenging an Orwellian Big Brother. Returning to Apple, Jobs contributed to the "Think Different" ads, celebrating the misfits and rebels, emphasizing that those who believe they can change the world often do.

Staying hungry means always wanting to learn and get better. Leaders and business folks need to stay curious, keep seeking new ideas, and not be okay with how things are – always room to improve.

Being foolish is about taking risks and not always following the usual rules. Leaders should be okay with trying new things, even if it seems a bit crazy. Mistakes happen, but learning from them is key. It's also important to stay humble, realizing even experienced people can benefit from a bit of innocence when chasing groundbreaking ideas.

So, leaders should tackle problems with both determination and humility. This mindset encourages curiosity and boldness, understanding that success often involves facing the unknown.

In the changing business world, those who follow this "Stay Hungry, Stay Foolish" idea are better at leading with new ideas and bouncing back from challenges. Keeping that hunger for knowledge and daring to be a bit foolish in uncertain times sets the stage for creativity, adaptability, and, in the end, success.

Know Both the Big Picture and the Details

Jobs loved tackling big and small issues with passion. Some CEOs are great at big visions, others are detailed managers. Jobs was both. Time Warner CEO Jeff Bewkes said Jobs could see the big picture and focus on tiny design details. In 2000, he envisioned the personal computer as a "digital hub" for managing music, videos, and photos, leading to the iPod and iPad. In 2010, he shifted to the cloud strategy, building a server farm for seamless content syncing.

Jobs saw himself as a humanities person who liked electronics. Inspired by Edwin Land of Polaroid, he aimed to bridge humanities and sciences. He linked humanities to sciences, creativity to technology, and arts to engineering. While not the top technologist or designer, he uniquely blended poetry and processors, guided by intuitive business strategy.

His ability to connect humanities and sciences fascinated biographers like me, exploring Franklin and Einstein. This fusion, essential for creative economies, embodies applied imagination. Jobs, even in his final days, aimed to disrupt more industries, envisioning artistic textbooks and magical tools for photography and simplified, personal television. His success rules will keep Apple at the creative-tech intersection as long as Jobs's DNA remains at its core.

Leaders and business minds can draw valuable lessons from how Steve Jobs approached his work and innovation. Jobs wasn't just about grand ideas; he was a hands-on leader who knew the significance of details. In the realm of leadership, this dual perspective is crucial.

Firstly, it's about having a big vision. Jobs imagined the personal computer evolving into a central hub for managing various aspects of a user's life. For leaders, having a clear, overarching strategy is vital. It's about understanding the broader picture, figuring out where your company or project fits into the larger scheme. This vision gives a sense of direction, purpose, and a pathway for growth.

Secondly, paying attention to details is key. While envisioning the future, Jobs also cared about the shape and color of screws inside the iMac. This meticulous focus on finer points lays the foundation for excellence in design and user experience. Leaders should not only set the vision but also ensure that the execution meets the highest standards.

Jobs's blend of humanities and sciences is another important lesson. Leaders can adopt this by cultivating diverse teams that bring varied perspectives to the table.

Additionally, Jobs's knack for adapting and disrupting industries, even towards the end, teaches leaders to be forward-thinking. Embracing change and maintaining innovation are crucial in today's dynamic business world. Whether it's transforming textbooks into artistic creations or simplifying digital photography, the drive to revolutionize and enhance should always be present.

Innovative Leapfrogging

Let's have a closer look at how Steve Jobs went about things when the iMac needed to add music features. He didn't just play catch-up but he played it smart. Instead of just improving the iMac's CD drive, he jumped head first into it. Thinking "Why not reinvent the music game wholesale?". He introduced iTunes, the digital download purchasing service and a friendly music player called simply, the iPod. This was not about playing catch up but rather to leapfrog ahead with a new approach.

Jobs did not settle for being in second place; he wanted to be at the head of others. He didn't just play catch-up when the iMac couldn't take on in the music scene, he redefined an entirely new game. Instead of a basic improvement, he turned things around with iTunes, the iTunes Store and then with the help of an mp3 player invented Universal Music's Apple iPod. It was like jumping ahead with a different vibe altogether.

Product Over Profits

This is the period when they were making the original Macintosh, where Jobs was not interested in tightening his belt or counting funding. No, it was all about something that would simply be amazingly shocking. But he directed his team to action with the goal of making it "insanely great", not fretting over revenue or shaving off costs.

Jobs would likely have paid a little more for it; no, it did result in one or two speed bumps but he thought that his goal was to try and achieve the right balance of wealth – if you pour all your soul into something subs Work will pay.

80s and Jobs was with his team designing Macintosh, the first one of its kind. By doing so he wasn't setting eyes on whatever revenue was being rolled out. He wasn't giving the idea that, "Hey let's save some pennies here." Not really at all. The sentiment was more akin to, "Let's do something so ridiculously awesome we just don't care about pushing it through with even half as many profits or whether this costs us 10 cents cheaper than before." They just wanted to pour all their love into getting it right so that they could end up with something incredible.

Was it worth the extra funds, and was that pretty rocky ride a bit of a pain? Of course not – you see if Jobs had this big scheme all worked out in his head "alright guys we are going to squirrel away cash now for our beautiful Macintosh computer then once we're ready with an amazing product which everyone can afford me is open in Greece.

Hence, let's discuss how exactly Jobs perceived the equilibrium between creation of a masterpiece and making money? Picture this: in 1984, that was when the Macintosh project became a company within Steve's organization and started producing products in earnest during NeXT's early days. Jobs wasn't sitting across the table with a calculator, fretting about gains. No way. He wanted to tell his team-insanely great Macintosh. Disregard low costs, forget about the financial tricks.

That's why all the talk was about creating something that would make you fall jaw. Yeah, it might have been slightly more expensive and yes sent a few chills down along the way. But Jobs saw this magic formula – to invest all he had on making something unbelievable and the money was bound to follow suit.

Intuition Over Focus Groups

When Steve Jobs took his team for a retreat to discuss the original Macintosh, someone inquired whether they should conduct some market research so that it knows what customers want. Jobs said, "No, because customers don't know what they want until we show them. He referred to a Henry Ford story who stated that if he had asked the customer, they would have probably wanted a faster horse."

Jobs did not always ask customers, it was more important to care deeply about their needs, even more so with intuition and instinct to understand desires before they were expressed. He designed this intuition during his study of Buddhism philosophy in India desiring the values based on wisdom through experience. Jobs often acted like a focus group as one-man creators of products for himself and his friends.

For example, in 2000 there were many portable music players but Jobs, a lover of music, thought they sucked. He desired a simple gadget that could fit in his pocket to store about one thousand songs, which then gave birth to the iPod. "We made the iPod for ourselves," he said, "and when you're doing something for yourself, or your best friend or family, you're not going to cheese out".

Bend Reality

Jobs' ability to get people delirious doing the impossible was familiarly known as his Reality Distortion Field, named after an episode of Star Trek in which aliens create a reality so real and convincing that even humans can't tell it. For an early instance, when Jobs was working on the night shift at Atari and encouraged Steve Wozniak to make a game called Breakout. Wozniak said it was going to take months, but Jobs looked at him and insisted he could pull that off in four days. Wozniak knew that was unfeasible, but he ended up doing it anyway.

People who had not come across Jobs considered the Reality Distortion Field as a polite term for bullying and lying. But those who worked with him confessed that this, so annoying as it could be, made them do almost impossible things.

Since Jobs felt that life's usual procedures were not meant for him, he could inspire his team to alter the course of computer history with a pittance compared to what Xerox or IBM had. "It was a self-fulfilling distortion," says Debi Coleman, who also worked with the Mac team and won an award one year for being the best employee at holding her ground against Jobs. "You did the impossible, simply because you didn't know it was impossible."

One day Jobs walked into Larry Kenyon, the engineer who was working on the Macintosh Operating System cubicle and said that it is taking too long to boot up. Kenyon was beginning to speak as to why the boot up time could not be reduced when Jobs interrupted him. "Could you trim 10 seconds off the boot time to save a life?" he inquired. Kenyon admitted that he probably could.

Jobs wrote on a whiteboard and demonstrated that if there were five million people using the Mac kind of computer, it took them 10 seconds longer to turn it back in each day. So hundreds or more hours went by just for switching off PCs? Well, 365 days every year let's say three hundred fifty millions are about at least one century lifetimes within an entire year. Finally after a few weeks Kenyon was able to boot up the machine in 28 seconds less.

When designing the iPhone, Jobs decided that he wanted its face to be a delicate and scratch proof glass instead of plastic. He visited Wendell Weeks, the head of Corning who informed him that his company had come up with a chemical exchange process in the 1960s which resulted in what they referred to as Gorilla glass. Jobs requested for an immediate shipment of a huge consignment of Gorilla glass after six months and shockingly, Weeks put him down saying he hadn't made it- "Don't be afraid," Jobs replied.

This shocked Weeks, who did not know about Jobs' Reality Distortion Field. He tried to point out that a fake self-assurance could not surmount the difficulties of engineering, but Jobs had proven on numerous occasions that he doesn't accept this notion.

He started unblinking at Weeks. He said, "yes you can do it". "Get your mind around it". "We did it in under six months," he says, "we put our best scientists and engineers on this to be sure that we just made things work!" Now every piece of glass used for iPhones or an iPad is produced in America by Corning.

Tolerate Only "A" Players

Jobs was quick-tempered, rude and hard towards the people around him. However, the way he treated people although not very commendable was a result of his quest for perfection and willingness to work with only the best. It was his way to avoid what he called "the bozo explosion," where managers were so polite that mediocre people felt comfortable saying around.

He said, "I don't think I run roughshod over people," but if something sucks he tells them to their faces. "It was my job to be honest." When I asked whether such results would have been possible while being nicer, he said maybe they could have. "But I am not that person," he said. Maybe there's a nicer way —a gentlemen's club where we all wear ties and speak in the Brahmin language; velvet code words—but I don't know that way because I am middle-class from California .

Was all his stormy and abusive conduct essential? Probably not. He could have inspired his team in other ways. "I love being calmer and not fighting over everything. I think a company can be a good family." But then he added something that is undeniably true: "If I had run the Macintosh project, it would probably be a mess".

Important is to recognize that Jobs's rudeness and ruggedness were also coupled with the capability of being inspiring. He filled Apple employees with a long-term desire to build revolutionary products and the certainty that they were able to do what was considered unimaginable.

"We have to judge him by the result". Jobs had a close-knit family, and so it was at Apple: His best players usually stayed on longer and were more loyal than others at other companies, including ones run by kinder and gentler bosses. CEOs who during the study of Jobs decide to follow his roughness without understanding how he could instill loyalty make an unhealthy mistake.

"Over the years I've learned that when you have really good people, they don't need hand-holding," said Jobs. "By planning for greatness you will achieve it". Most of them agree with it. "People would tell me, Debi Coleman recalls, how do you work with that asshole?" "But I really felt like the luckiest person in the world to have worked with him".

Push for Perfection

When developing almost every product he ever came up with, Jobs would "pause" at one point and start his work again from the beginning because something wasn't quite right. Even the movie Toy Story happened. Jeff Katzenberg and the crew at Disney, which had acquired rights to the movie, pushed the Pixar team.

It was until Steve Jobs and director John Lasseter decided to end production of this flick so he rewrote it to be more friendlier. He and his store guru Ron Johnson suddenly decided to postpone everything for a few months so the layouts of stores could be restructured not by product categories, but rather activities.

The same applied to the iPhone. The first design had the glass screen installed in an aluminum case. On a Monday morning Jobs went to see Ive. He said, "I didn't sleep last night because I realized that I just do not love it." To his regret Jobs was correct; he saw this instantly. "I remember I was feeling completely ashamed that he had to note it," he stated. The issue was that the iPhone should have been all about the display, but in this design it had a case that vied with and competed against instead of giving way to the screen.

The whole device felt more masculine, task-oriented and efficient. "Guys, you have literally killed yourselves in creating this design for the past nine months, but here there is a fundamental change," Jobs told Ive's team.

A similar occurrence was as Jobs and Ive were completing the iPad. Jobs at one time looked at the model and seemed a little displeased. It did not appear easy and jovial enough to pick up and carry away. They had to demonstrate that you could reach out with a one-handed grab, spontaneously.

They thought that the lower edge should be slightly bowed so a user could simply grab it without worrying about picking it up very carefully. It also meant that engineering had to elaborate the required connection ports and buttons in a thin, simple lip that gently sloped away at its base. The product was held up until that change could be made.

Even the hidden sides of Jobs's perfectionism. He had already helped his father to install a fence around their backyard when he was young and they were instructed that even the rear of it needed as much attention as its front.

"Nobody will ever know," Steve said. His father answered, "But you will know, a true craftsman uses a good piece of wood even for the back of a cabinet against the wall". His father explained to them that they should do this as well – not waste their material but use it effectively. Such passion for perfection was the sign of an artist.

Jobs used this lesson in managing the Apple II and Macintosh by focusing on what was inside. They both headed back to align the chips neatly in order that the board would be good-looking. This was very strange to the engineers of Macintosh, because Jobs had mandated that this machine be made highly airtight. "Nobody is going to see the PC board," one of them protested.

Jobs reacted as his father had: "I want it to be as beautiful as possible even if I put it in the box. No classy woodworker is going to mark the back of a cabinet with crummy material, even though no one will see it," He said this was because they were genuine artists and thus should behave as such. And when the board was redesigned, he made his engineers and fellow members of the Macintosh team sign them so that their names could be engraved inside the case. "True artists mark their products," he said.

Imagine treading in the footsteps of giants, following an enduring trail left by one of the most influential personalities on both sides of technology and leadership – Steve Jobs. His path goes beyond the parameters of invention, touching upon areas such as passion, determination and unwavering pursuit for perfection.

"Your work is going to fill a large part of your life, and the only way to be truly satisfied is to do what you believe is great" he once said. This philosophy is a rallying call for leaders to attach passion into every task. It is the engine that hurls us over and beyond challenges to achieve extraordinary successes. It is in the furnace of passion that ideas do not arise, but they get developed from being shaped to coming alive with a spark added onto them which can turn everyday things into marvels.

"I didn't see it then, but I realized later on that being fired from Apple was the best thing that ever happened to me," reflected Jobs. In this crucible of negative events – setbacks and seeming failures were not roadblocks for Jobs. It served as stepping-stones for greater heights." It is in adversity that strength and resilience are developed, leading all the way to innovation and triumph.

Throughout his story, we found Jobs highlighting design thinking – a way of life that transformed industry for technology. He declared, "Design is not just what it looks like and feels like. Design is how it works." This insight encourages leaders to take on a users-based perspective, designing solutions that do not only fulfill but surpass the demands of their customers.

The fact that Jobs was able to see what the future holds and steered his team in its direction is indicative of inspiring leadership. We are called to develop a mindset that dares to dream beyond the usual, motivating our teams towards their goals of reaching out for stars. Visionary leadership is more than foresight, it requires strategic thinking and the ability to pursue innovative paths despite being met with skepticism in its early stages. It is about breaking the status quo and discovering a path into uncharted waters.

Where Jobs led the Apple ecosystem thrived through a culture that valued excellence. "Be a yardstick of quality. Some people aren't used to an environment where excellence is expected," he declared. There, call to leaders the development of cultures that nurture excellence – set high standards challenging the status quo and drive continuous improvement along with developing a sense of pride and ownership amongst teams. It is in societies where excellence prevails that individuals and organizations flourish, breaking the borders of what should have been possible.

Such elements as simplicity both in communication and product design became characteristics of Jobs' leadership style. He believed, "Simplicity is the ultimate sophistication." In today's complicated world, leaders are admonished to take heed of this piece of advice. Simple communication means that messages are straightforward, and simple product design indicates intuitiveness. With simplicity and elegance, is where leaders find a very powerful instrument of efficient communication as well as user engagement.

Jobs had a high regard for the intersection of art and technology. He declared this way "It's in Apple's DNA that technology alone is not enough— it's technology married with liberal arts, married with the humanities that yields us." It is fundamental from recognizing the symbiotic relationship between art and technology. Innovation means more than just doing things better, it is about creating emotional experiences and integrating technology into the essence of being human.

CHAPTER 3

The Power of Crisis: How Great Leaders Survive

Crises really hit organizations hard, affecting every part of their existence. It's not just about disruptions; it's like a ripple effect that touches everything. First off, financially, it can mess up an organization's money situation. Market ups and downs, problems with how things run, and spending more to handle the crisis can mess with profits and shake up the financial stability. This might lead to people losing their jobs, budgets getting slashed, or the organization restructuring to get back on its feet.

Then there's the reputation side of things. A crisis can seriously affect how people see an organization. When things go south during a crisis, it can really damage an organization's reputation. If the handling of the crisis isn't spot on, the damage can stick around for a long time.

Getting people to trust the organization again is a slow process. It's not just about customers; even investors and everyone else start questioning what's going on. Even those big-name brands that everyone usually trusts find themselves facing a heap of doubt. It's like you have to start from scratch to build that trust back up.

Inside the organization, a crisis can mess with the way people work together. Employees get stressed out dealing with uncertainty and fear. How the leaders handle things and communicate makes a big difference in how everyone feels and how productive they are. After the crisis, there might be changes in how the organization is set up or how things are done, as they learn from what happened.

On the strategic side, a crisis makes organizations rethink how they handle risks and have backup plans. Going through a crisis can push an organization to be more innovative and adaptable. It makes them think about what really matters and be more aware of what could go wrong. Oddly enough, successfully dealing with a crisis can make an organization stronger, ready to face whatever comes next.

When a crisis hits, the people making decisions in organizations have to deal with a lot of uncertainty and confusion. It's a real mental challenge. The pressure goes up as leaders have to make important choices with things changing fast. They're dealing with complex situations, looking at risks, and thinking about how their decisions will affect things in the long run.

Additionally, the psychological stress of crisis situations can cause decision fatigue among organizational leaders which reduces their ability to make high-quality decisions. Studies show that chronic stress can negatively affect cognitive functions, impairing attention, memory and problem-solving.

In the organizational setting, this cognitive fatigue may lead to decisions not fully optimal because leaders cannot sustain their level of analytical rigor and strategic foresight in moments of crises.

The procedural dimension of organizational decision-making also gets major changes when a crisis occurs. The decision-making models that are traditionally structured and linear may prove to be less effective in the event of a crisis characterized by urgency or complexity. The process of decision making also changes from being too rigid to adaptive and agile approaches in times of crisis, organizations becoming more flexible.

Such procedural changes triggered by crisis are characterized by the need for fast processing of information and decentralized decision making. The stable environments where working in hierarchical decision-making frameworks is prevalent might be replaced by collaborative and cross-functional teams with shared responsibility for addressing the multidimensional challenges of the crisis.

The transition towards collaborative decision-making is caused by the understanding that only a variety of viewpoints and skill sets helps to survive in utterly new circumstances.

In addition, the temporal dimension of decision-making changes throughout a crisis. The pressure to respond quickly may result in the adoption of shorter decision cycles by organizations, where real-time information and immediate action is deemed crucial. Apart from allowing organizations to react quickly, this deviation from what is normally involved in making such decisions can be both positive and negative as it may result in superficial decision-making.

During a crisis, organizations may develop adaptive decision-making strategies in the crucible of such crises. For instance scenario planning becomes a useful functionality as it allows organizations to envision several potential futures and prepare flexible strategies that can be adapted depending on how the happenings unfold. This proactive approach to decision-making enables organizations to stay one step ahead and reduce the effects of uncertainty.

Additionally, decision-making under conditions of crisis frequently involves a switch in attitude toward risk. Organizations may be forced to take calculated risks in order to steer themselves out of the crisis successfully. This turning away from the risk-averse dynamics calls for a delicate balance between embracing innovation and its potential fallouts, thus underlining that decision making at times of crisis should always be highly nuanced.

The effect of a crisis on organizational decision-making is not merely confined to internal processes but includes communicating and transparently. As organizations must communicate their decisions effectively and transparently to both internal and external stakeholders during crises, effective communication becomes a linchpin. Accurate information should be disseminated widely to help protect trust and ensure that the organization's actions are worthwhile in terms of their alignment with its values.

Nevertheless, the problem is to find a balance between transparency and concern about possible panic or undesirable effects. Organizational leaders need to navigate this difficult terrain providing the right amount of information that is enough to establish confidence but not too much as it can cause unnecessary alarm. Facilitating the ability to communicate decisively and transparently becomes a distinctive feature of good crisis disaster decision-making.

While crisis situations present tremendous obstacles, they also offer incredibly unique opportunities for organizational learning and development. After the crisis, post-crisis assessments become necessary parts of decision making processes in organizations that help them examine how effective their responses to a given crisis were and what needs improvements. A reflective decision-making process helps organizations develop resilience, and as such future crises would be informed by the lessons learnt during this particular one.

Identifying and Examining the Various Sources that Contribute to Crises within Organizations

The challenges that organizations may face can be taken away from Churchill's leadership during one of the most turbulent times in history. Churchill's wartime leadership story shows multiple vital sources of crisis and the ways they were addressed.

Churchill became the head of state during one of the most turbulent times in history. The shadow of Nazi Germany's peril hung over Europe and Britain became the target for a looming battle. Internal factors such as the missteps during early years of war point to events that trigger organizational crises. The lack of coordination in military planning and deficiencies in communication between different armed services made it necessary to emphasize the internal preparation.

One of the major sources of crisis that Churchill had to undergo was uncertainty in leadership. The fog of war meant that decisions had to be made in a hurry, sometimes based on imperfect information. This emulates the uncertainties faced by organizations, whether such challenges seep from economic slowdowns, technological disruptions or random market changes.

Leadership agility in the face of uncertainty illustrates a high level of leadership allegiance with Churchill able to make decisive decisions despite ambiguity.

Churchill's leadership during the Battle of Britain shows how organization stability depends on outside factors. The constant German bombings constituted an essential threat, similar to the challenges that organizations might face externally from factors such as worldwide economic recessions or industry-wide disturbances.

Churchill's inspirational speeches and unshaken grit rallied not only his country, but also stressed the role of communication in emergencies. Transparent communication emerges as a critical link for organizational resilience by instilling trust and cohesion even in the midst of hardships.

Another important aspect to take away is the strategic farsightedness of Churchill. He understood the need for adaptability and a focus on innovation, supporting new technologies such as radar that proved to be critical in flipping the war. This reflects the need for organizations to keep innovating and morphing with circumstances in order to conquer them.

Second, resilience in the face of defeat becomes evident when considering Churchill's leadership. The evacuation from Dunkirk serves as a symbol of his ability to transform what appeared at the moment an unfavorable situation into a retreat in tactical fashion that kept intact British core military might. Crisis-struck organizations can be inspired by the Churchill spirit, learning how to adjust and come back stronger after failure.

External Shocks

In the realm of organizational management, external shocks are a potent force that poses significant challenges way beyond the bounds of predictability. Natural disasters, pandemics and political upheavals that can affect or terminate the viability of organizations. However, this introduction prefaces a discussion on how such external shocks outside an organization's remit can reverberate through operations and supply chains upending the bastion of monetary equilibrium.

One of the most notable incidents involving an external shock that led to a broad organizational crisis is associated with COVID-19, which originated in late 2019. The novelty of the pandemic did not only reflect weaknesses in terms of public health care systems, but also created reverberations through the global business environment. The lockdowns, the disruptions in supply chains and changes to consumer behavior were a unique challenge for organizations across sectors that had very little warning.

The demand fell dramatically, the production was stopped and global supply chains were disrupted in most businesses that resulted in significant financial burden. For instance, the travel and hospitality industries suffered devastating losses due to grounded airlines, closed hotels, and vanished tourism.

Companies dependent on brick-and mortar, physical retail suffered greatly in these lockdown times as the result of closures and changed consumer behavior towards online shopping. The automotive industry, which was already struggling, faced another debacle when production facilities were shut down while also seeing its consumer spending drained.

The pandemic also affected the workforce significantly. The digital world became even more important for many workers, challenging the technology and logistics. Organizations had to re-engineer quickly in the new ways of collaboration, and such issues as productivity, employee wellness influenced the organization culture. In the industries in which it was impossible to work remotely, however, there were different issues with safety and disruptions of operations.

The vulnerabilities of the supply chain were exposed when companies understood just how much they had become reliant on certain areas or vendors. The shortage of essential components and raw materials showed the weaknesses in intricate global chain supplies. Companies worked to counteract shortages, delays and looked for alternatives in nature of supply chains which could bolster their ability to withstand future disruptions.

Besides directly operational issues, the pandemic introduced a significant change in consumer behaviors. The process of digital transformation accelerated due to the rapid growth witnessed in e-commerce. Firms that had invested in strong online portals were better placed to sail through the storm, while ones trailing behind faced an increased battle for survival.

Another example of an external shock hitting society is the 2008 global financial crisis. The crisis, which emerged from the failure of many big financial companies as well as a deep economic recession that spanned industries, was far reaching. Insolvency loomed for financial institutions, and governments had to take extraordinary bailouts in a move aimed at restoring soundness of the systems.

In the automotive sector, however, there were some tough times ahead as consumer confidence sank low resulting in reduced spending and very sharp decline of vehicle sales. The timeless companies like

General Motors and Chrysler were brought to the brink of bankruptcy, which largely destroyed their ability for survival without government support. This crisis helped to demonstrate the interdependence of international financial markets and industries' susceptibility towards systemic shocks.

The world economy had its turning point when a financial crisis hit in 2008. Then the housing market collapsed, when financial giants stood on verge of catastrophic failure, people remained wondering as to how all this could have occurred. During this challenging period, one man stood up as an agent of wisdom and stability. Warren Buffet, the famous investor and chief executive at Berkshire Hathaway.

As the crisis kept intensified, it aroused enormous public interest in Buffett's ideas and beliefs but most of all his advice on how to steer through such troubled waters was sought after. This piece focuses on Warren Buffett's commentary on the financial crisis of 2008 investments he made during that period and how his inputs played a major role in steering the evolution of the economy.

Warren Buffett is known for his long-term investing philosophy and ability to weather market fluctuations. Prior to the financial calamity of 2008, he had been a harsh critic on the housing sector and cautioned about perils emanating from subprime mortgages. Once he noted in a 2003 interview with CNBC, "I can almost say that there will be an unstable situation and it may come next week or the following month."

However, as the crisis progressed, Buffett adopted a more cautious stance by assessing investment opportunities periodically. During the crisis, he spectacularly invested $ 5 billion into Goldman Sachs to give it a lift of confidence thought to be on its deathbed.

Even in the midst of the crisis, Buffett was positive about the long term future of the economy. In an interview that he granted to Charlie Rose in 2008, he stated," We will not have depression. It is recession only and the American public as well as their businesses are very strong, hence; they shall be restored back fast."

Rethinking the crisis, Buffett has stressed long-term vision which prevented him from being swept away by market craze. More importantly, he had also highlighted the importance of a strong capital base for financial institutions so that they can withstand future crises. In this interview with CNBC in 2013, he said that "if you are not operating from a business where significant fixed assets have been created then one ought to provide for surplus capital. And if you don't have it, you're not going to be around."

When the financial crisis struck, Warren Buffett made some investments that were considered courageous. One of the biggest was his investment in $5 billion Goldman Sachs, which he invested during September 2008 when the crisis came to climax. In its announcement last year, Buffett said he was a fan of Goldman Sachs from the first time that he purchased stocks in the company during the early 1990s. He believed it to be one of the finest investment banking firms in the world.

Buffett also invested in other companies that were suffering due to the crisis. In October 2008, he spent $3 billion on General Electric and furthered his position in the company. In 2011, he also invested

$10.7 billion in IBM that was severely affected by the crisis.

There were several factors that made Buffett invest in these places. He believed in the future of those companies. He has always served as a value investor seeking companies that are significantly undervalued but have great potential to grow. Another factor was the market turbulence that came with a crisis.

With many investors scared and selling securities outright, the value hunters including Buffett got themselves some bargains as stocks of certain companies sold off sharply.

All things considered, these have proven to be good investments for Buffet. Since the crisis, Goldman Sachs and General Electric have bounced back higher than they were in earlier investments. He has also been successful in his investment in IBM, as the stocks have more than doubled since he invested. Since the crisis, such investments have helped Berkshire Hathaway perform well.

As the financial crisis of 2008 took its toll, Warren Buffett and Berkshire Hathaway made various investments in struggling institutions to shore up their positions during this period. However, the most prominent one was the $5 billion investment in Goldman Sachs announced in 2008. This investment, which was in the form of preferred shares, gave Goldman Sachs required capital when necessary at a time when the company faced serious financial predicaments.

This was evident in Buffett's investment into Goldman Sach that was viewed as an approval to the failing financial corporation and it stabilized his stock price together with investor confidence. The investment was complemented by an attractive dividend yield of 10%, which guaranteed Berkshire Hathaway a steady flow of income.

In contrast to the investment made to Goldman Sachs, Berkshire Hathaway also invested in other financial institutions such as General Electric and Bank of America during the crisis. The capital and income of Berkshire Hathaway came from these investments, Goldman Sachs preferred stock.

In general, the goal of such investments was to finance and secure financial establishments that lacked support during the crisis. Through these investments, Buffett was able to benefit from good valuations and help bolster the wider economy. As a rule, these investments have been profitable for Berkshire Hathaway as the companies involved gradually emerged from the crisis and performed well in the years thereafter.

In both the COVID-19 pandemic and the financial crisis of 2008, organizations faced difficulties that went beyond immediate fiscal ramifications. This became the focus of reputational risks, leadership scrutiny and strategic reassessment. Crises, whether based on external shocks or internal aspects, point to the necessity of effective crisis management strategies.

After such crises, successful organizations displayed resilience through adaptive practices. They expanded supply chains, technology infrastructure and they embodied innovation. The crises acted as catalysts for quick transformations that compelled organizations to reimagine the traditional business models and embrace agile, futuristic approaches.

These instances demonstrate the randomness of external shocks and a necessity for an organization to make adaptability its core competency. The crises represent some of the greatest threats to survival but also offer opportunities for organizational rebirth and growth. Capacity to get through external shocks better is great proof of leadership, farsightedness practices and a strong organizational culture.

Poor Leadership and Governance

Theranos was all about a big medical breakthrough, guided by Elizabeth Holmes, a leader with charisma and vision. But as things played out, it turned out that the cool medical innovation story was actually a mix of lies and mistakes.

Leadership is about integrity, the moral guide in decision-making. Holmes' journey into poor leadership started with a lack of ethics. The overstated claims about Theranos' abilities weren't just false; they jeopardized the health of people relying on accurate medical tests. This departure from ethical responsibility not only tarnished

Holmes' personal image but also the company's reputation.

Leadership is also about accountability, and governance plays a vital role in upholding that. At Theranos, ineffective governance allowed unchecked power in Holmes' hands. The board, captivated by the promise of innovation, failed to scrutinize the leadership. This lack of checks allowed the unchecked spread of false narratives.

The erosion of identity is a gradual process. As Holmes got deeper into deception, she distanced herself from the values that should define a leader. The stark contrast between Theranos' mission and its reality showcased the unraveling of identity for both Holmes and the company.

Poor leadership and governance result in a credibility crisis. In Theranos' case, once the truth surfaced, the damage was irreparable. The public had believed in a revolutionary technology, only to discover it was built on lies. Regaining credibility is tough once lost, affecting not just the leader but the entire organization.

A leader's identity is tied to the organization's reputation. Holmes, once seen as a visionary, had her identity tarnished with the truth about Theranos. Credibility became synonymous with deception and failure. It's a reminder that leadership is about delivering promises with honesty and transparency.

Theranos' downfall is a stark example of poor leadership consequences. It underscores the importance of ethics, accountability, and oversight in maintaining personal and organizational identity. The aftermath of Theranos serves as a cautionary tale, urging leaders to prioritize values over superficial success and recognize that losing identity and credibility can be swift and severe without principled leadership and governance.

In any successful organization, having effective leaders and good governance is crucial. They play a key role in shaping the organization's path and ensuring it keeps growing. On the flip side, if leadership is lacking, it can lead to a bunch of problems that affect the whole organization.

The main issue here is weak leadership, which goes beyond just being not good at the job. A leader faces problems when there's no clear plan, bad decisions are made, and unethical behavior happens. If these issues aren't addressed, they can spread in the organization, leading to a tough-to-stop downward spiral.

A crucial part of being a good leader is creating a clear and motivating plan. Leaders should be like architects, mapping out a route for the organization to follow. In cases of weak leadership, this plan might be unclear or missing altogether, leaving employees feeling lost. Without a clear path, decisions get messy, and the organization drifts without purpose, missing chances and struggling with problems.

Bad decision-making often shows up when leaders can't make tough choices. Whether it's because they can't decide, make bad calls, or avoid dealing with hard problems, these failures can cause a lot of issues. Without strong leadership making clear choices, problems stick around, and chances slip by. The organization gets stuck in constant indecision, making it hard to adapt to a changing business world.

Financial Mismanagement

Financial mismanagement is a multi-faceted threat to organizations and can be as grave as financial disasters like fraud or embezzlement, unsustainable business operations that have left many big enterprises bankrupt. The consequences of these problems are not limited to finance but go deeper and influence the entire well being and stability of an organization.

Financial mismanagement is partly attributed to decision-making deficiencies in financial matters. Such decisions are made by executives and financial leaders without performing detailed analyses or reflecting on the matter in a long-term perspective. This failure to focus on the future leads ultimately to inappropriate investments, mistargeting resources and a lack of perceptiveness regarding market trends. Basically, a poorly outlined financial plan may lay the ground for precarious finances.

Yet another face of financial mismanagement that poses enormous risks to organizations are fraud and embezzlement. Fraudulent transactions whether perpetrated by internal or external actors remain unnoticed for a prolonged time and cost millions of dollars. Modern financial fraud is too sophisticated for organizations to rely on inadequate internal controls and only occasionally assess their effectiveness at preventing treasonous acts.

Weak business approach only makes the challenges of financial mismanagement grow even bigger. Organizations can exhibit behaviors that favor short-term benefits over sustainable success. For instance, cost reduction at the expense of quality control may give monetary rewards initially but in due course will lead to loss of reputation and legal implications as well. Oppositely, a sustainable business would take the effects over financial health and reputation among stakeholders in consideration.

Poor risk management is, therefore, an important element of poor financial control. While operating in dynamic environments, organizations must be watchful enough to detect risk detection, evaluation and management. Without a well-developed risk management framework, an organization is vulnerable to external shocks and market instabilities that can compromise financial stability.

This is one of the common mistakes that organizations may commit, especially while trying to expand and deal with short-term financial concerns in terms of overreliance on debt. Although debt can be an excellent financial tool, excessive dependence on it without a well-thought plan to pay back could result in the vicious cycle of debts when payments become uncontrollable. However, smart financial management balances the capital structure between equity and debt to ensure that a stable base is achieved.

The effects of financial mismanagement are not limited to the realm of the finances; they extend across an organization. When the company cannot invest in professional development programs because of financial instability, employee morale and productivity can decrease through downsizing or salary cuts. If stakeholder trust is lost, be it of customers or investors and business partners some there can also take decades to restore the reputation.

To overcome these barriers, organizations need to emphasize on financial literacy and competency at all levels. All the executives and financial leaders should have a thorough understanding of finance concepts that they need to revisit, time after time, for overcoming changing economic structures. Moreover, creating a culture of accountability is necessary in fraud prevention and detection.

Operational Failures

The Challenger Space Shuttle with proposed launch date January 28, 1986 approached a fatal failure only seventy-three seconds into its flight killing all seven crew members aboard. The disaster occurred because of a fatal design failure in the shuttle's solid rocket boosters. However, cold temperatures that were considerably lower than normal on the morning of launch caused the O-rings made from rubber to harden and lose flexibility as intended in moving joints within boosters.

The origin of the operational failure can be found in the pre-launch decision making processes. The engineers at Morton Thiokol, the contractor for solid rocket boosters, said that they were concerned about the O-rings' effect in cold weather. But under mounting pressure to continue the launch and dissonant information, they gave in to organizational and external demands. The go-ahead decision that was made despite reservations, became the turning point in time leading up to the tragedy.

Challenger disaster shows how ignoring operational concerns instead of following external pressure leads to accidental consequences. First of all, the failure was not a mere technical malfunction; it pertained to decision-making issues as well as communication and organizational procedures. Similarly, the communication failure between engineers and management as well as ineffective risk communications contributed significantly to this crisis.

The Challenger disaster also made it clear that organizational culture was responsible for silencing dissidents. The engineers who raised concerns over the O-rings were met with resistance and could not communicate their message effectively. This characteristic of the crisis underlines that an organizational culture should encourage open communication and value all team members' participation, no matter their position in the hierarchy.

The fallout from the Challenger incident included emergence of Rogers Commission, a body headed by William P.Rogers former U.S Secretary The commission undertook a broad study on reasons leading to the operational failure, namely not only technical shortcomings but also systematic issues with NASA decision-making mechanisms.

The results stressed the importance of a cultural change within an organization that would result in giving more attention to safety and create conditions where invalid opinions are not only heard but seriously taken into consideration.

Operational failures within an organization may create fertile ground for crises, with consequences which can extend to various aspects of the operations These are 'breakdowns' which encompass a wide range of issues, from technological failures to supply chain disruptions and quality control lapses. To understand the magnitude of such operational glitches it is essential to explore in detail how modern business interactions intertwine.

Often, technological failures are to blame for the downfall of an operation; they can render any organization dysfunctional. From obsolete systems thinking to software bugs and hardware failures, these breakdowns are capable of disturbing important processes. In a digital age where operations rely on the web for information, these effects can extend to different elements of communication and data-based systems. The cascading factor in technical failure is often worsened by ineffective investment on resilient IT infrastructure which manifests this need for constant maintenance and improvement.

Supply chain disruptions are another dangerous aspect of operational failures. In the time of global commerce, organizations depend on complex webs of suppliers and partners to deliver an uninterrupted supply chain. Any interruption in this complex dance whether political, natural or unexpected disease waves through the whole operational environment. The ripple effect can emerge as delayed production, increased costing and the compromised ability to procure customer orders that might lessen its reputation.

Since many enterprises have the Achilles' heel of quality control issues, which multiplies this challenge. Poor quality products not only damage the confidence of consumers but also there are legal and financial risks. This requires an integrated approach that encompasses rigorous testing, adherence to guidelines set by the industry, and ongoing activities of improvement. Operational failures in quality control tend to stem from systemic problems, insufficient training or the shortsighted pursuit of speed rather than attention to long-term brand equity.

Processes that are dysfunctional – the silent enemy of organizational resilience - can turn everyday business as usual procedures into factories for crises. The above factors thwart agility and responsiveness with cumbersome workflows, redundant steps, bureaucratic bottlenecks. Modern business requires concise workflows that are dynamic enough to change with circumstances. Failure to address inefficiencies not only hinders day-to-day operations but also renders the organization helpless before unforeseen challenges.

Contingency planning seems to take the form of a foundation in reducing damages associated with operational misfortunes. What distinguishes success from complete failure is the ability to foresee such threats in advance and come up with a strategic action plan. Resiliency in planning calls for scenario analysis, risk evaluations and the preparation of response formats that are actionable. For organizations that do not pay much attention to this aspect, they keep panicking in crisis mode and only aggravate the initial operational failure.

What is equally important, there are appropriate response mechanisms. A timely and efficient reaction to operational errors presupposes transparent communication networks, strong definitions of roles, as well as a culture that implies honesty.

Uncoordinated response mechanisms during a crisis extend the duration of downtime, degrade reputation and cause financial ruin. Resilient organizations engage in team training, carry out periodic drills and encourage a spirit of flexibility to inhibit uncertainties.

Human Resources Issues

However, human resources issues are considered among the most sensitive and crucial elements of organizational dynamics that can either strengthen or destroy a company itself. Internal conflicts, labor strikes or allegations of harassment and talent management errors illustrate the running problems that tend to lead towards a crisis if not properly handled.

The essence lies not only in identifying these problems but also taking proactive measures to resolve them protecting employee's state of health as well organization integrity.

Divergent views, aspirations and ambitions converge in the crucible of internal organizational conflicts. These conflicts may originate from interpersonal clashes, differences in work styles or disagreements on strategic directives and if not handled with caution can lead to crisis. Conflict resolution requires an appreciation of the underlying conditions, open communication channels and a culture that values differing perspectives. Overlooking or minimizing disagreements within the team can lead to an unhealthy work climate, planting seeds of discontent that quickly eat away at group harmony and production.

Although portrayed as an age-old challenge to organizations, labor disputes often originate from the disparity of interests between management and employees. Specifically, these include compensation, working conditions and contractual issues that may cause resentments which might then lead to strikes or protests without proper management.

Being proactive with labor representatives, communicating openly about organization decisions can decrease the possible threat of potential labor disputes. A culture that appreciates the role of its workforce and creates a sense of collective goals is critical in minimizing conditions ripe for such conflicts.

Harassment allegations, which is a serious side of HR issues requires an approach zero tolerance and solid structure for prevention as well redressal. Harassment, which is either sexual, verbal or discriminative in nature can cause serious damages to people and may spoil the image of any organization. Preventive actions include the development of explicit anti-harassment policies, regular training sessions and promotion of a culture that supports respect and inclusivity. Prompt and fair investigations of allegations supported with suitable disciplinary measures uphold the desire for a secure, just workplace.

The lack of talent management is a less obvious but equally powerful challenge for human resources, which involves the careful recruitment and nurturing as well as keeping skilful individuals. Talent wars in competitive industries emphasize the importance of good talent management. Lack of high-potential employees, career development opportunities, skill gaps can lead to the talent flight creating losses in organizational abilities.

Active talent management refers to linking personal objectives with organizational targets, embracing a learning culture that is continuous and developing effective recruitment approaches in tandem with the direction of market forces.

Employee dissatisfaction – more than often a sign of human resources problems that may appear as lower production rates or high absenteeism, a malaise atmosphere in the organizational culture is another form it can take. To address the discontent, a holistic approach involving communication that works and employee engagement programs backed by timely transparent actions should be adopted.

Companies that value the well-being of their staff, create a positive working environment and provide channels through which dissatisfaction can be heard have an advantage in preventing discontent before it gets out of hand and becomes an overall crisis.

There is far more to human resource issues than just the short-term havoc that they may cause. These include unresolved conflicts, labor disputes, harassment claims and talent mismanagement that together can lead to an organization's toxic culture by hindering innovativeness and collaboration as well as preventing top-quality workers from joining or staying with the company.

Additionally, in times where corporate social responsibility is constantly monitored and ethical business methods are coming into focus more than ever before, mishandling human resources causes the damage to reputation that no good practice can undo.

Cyber Security Breaches

In the fast-paced and interdependent world of business today Technological dependence has given rise to an age where cybersecurity breaches present a potent threat. While they strive to optimize their operations through digitization, organizations are increasingly exposed not only to growing but also complex types of cyber threats.

The data breaches, hacking attempts and ransomware attacks can be seen as a powerful threat landscape that not only allows compromising vulnerable information but also interrupts vital functions and disrupts the reputation of an organization for good.

In the eye of this digital hurricane, data breaches become an imposing specter that can lead to a chain reaction sequence of post-breach reverberating effects. The contemporary world of business teems with large warehouses of sensitive information – customer data, company trade secrets, financial records and intellectual property all provide attractive targets for cybercriminals. This incursion not only threatens financial ruin but poses grave consequences for customer confidence, brand fidelity, and regulatory adherence.

The implications of a data breach go beyond the measurable outcomes, such as initial financial losses. They include the invisible, though highly impactful trust loss among clients. Customers, stakeholders and partners are now well aware of the weaknesses in safeguarding personal data. Not only does a breach reveal this weakness but it breaks down the implicit trust upon which any business-consumer relationship rests.

The repercussions are seen in lost customers, reputational carnage and sometimes long drawn out legal battles as organizations struggle to come to terms with the fact that their privacy has been compromised.

Hacking as a type of cybersecurity hazard is a persistent, dynamic danger that organizations ought to fight. Hacking can seek industrial espionage, money making to even serve ideological undertakings. The complexity of hacking methods combined with the complexities inherent to digital networks makes organizations vulnerable not only to unauthorized content, but also data manipulation and even intellectual property theft.

The cybersecurity organization's strategic imperative is not only about digital perimeter strengthening but a proactive stance that keeps an eye on emerging hacker strategies and anticipates potential threats.

Widespread ransomware attacks, a lethal aspect of cyber threats, are now crowned as powerful extortionists that lock up organizations. These attacks include the intrusion into systems together with key data encryption and ransom demands for its return. The repercussions of a successful ransomware attack go beyond the financial exploitation; they include operational disability, reputation landscapes as well as data loss.

Organizations end up in a classic catch-22 situation – accept the ransom and open themselves to further victimization or refuse it, but still suffer from productivity losses due to crippled operations.

The emergence of Internet of Things (IoT) and Cloud computing substantially enhances the cyber attack space by providing multiple platforms for threat actors. However, organizations do not only have to deal with protecting conventional IT infrastructures but also preventing countless interdependent devices. The intricacy of managing a variety of people's endpoints which may act as gateways for criminal elements highlights the need for holistic cybersecurity plans that transcend traditional perimeters.

In this uncertain terrain that organizations have to navigate, smart proactive and holistic approach becomes the seesaw of resilience. Strong cybersecurity frameworks do not only require implementation of advanced technology but also needs nurturing a culture fostering e-awareness among employees. The human factor, which is in most cases the weakest point of defense against cyberattacks needs constant training and education to strengthen organization's insusceptibility towards social engineering tactics and phishing attempts.

Acting upon the collaboration with cybersecurity specialists and using threat intelligence proves to be impossible without it. Organizations therefore need to do more than just strengthening their defenses but also putting in place an agile response mechanism that can quickly detect and respond when breaches materialize. Thus, cyber resilience is an integral element of a strategic imperative which must involve technology with the human resource and organizational culture.

Reputational Damage

The fragility of reputation in corporations is an evergreen topic, and with the onset of the digital age comes a higher intensity towards scrutiny as well as speed that damage can occur to reputations. A reputational crisis could therefore be said to arise from negative publicity, mistakes in general practitioners of relations or social media controversies that were not well considered and managed swiftly. Today, where perception counts so much and public sentiment can dictate the path of an institution; responsibility towards image is never greater.

Adverse publicity, usually occasioned by unexpected incidents or questions of proper conduct in some way, may stretch out a pall from an organization's reputation that long endures. It arises from a number of perils, like product recalls; ethical lapses; environmental issues and legal entanglements. In the age of digital revolution information spreads like wildfire; this is attributed to speed by which news whether accurate or mere sensationalism travels and organizations have very little time in trying to respond as well influence that narrative.

A powerful instance of bad publicity influencing reputation is the Deepwater Horizon oil spill event in 2010 that not only supplied devastating environmental harm but also unleashed a tsunami wave of unfavorable coverage for BP. However, not only BP's financial score but also its image as a responsible corporate citizen was forever ruined by the oppressive media coverage and public fury. This case is the perfect example of lasting damage that a company's image can suffer as a result of unwanted publicity.

Another dimension of reputational risk is public relations missteps which can magnify the damage arising from adverse media reports. The ways in which an organization communicates during a crisis, its degree of transparency and the ability to empathetically address concerns act as either mitigants or drivers for reputational damage. Various situations where organizations play down the seriousness of a situation providing inconsistent information or show an indifference to stakeholder concern only amplify reputational damage.

However, the United Airlines passenger removal scenario that occurred in 2017 serves as a prime example of what may result from mishaps during public relations. However, the company's initial response was harshly criticized as insensitive and devoid of any compassion.

A viral video showing an eviction of a passenger from an airplane caused the crisis to which United Airlines faced widespread condemnation and reputation loss. Other people would consider that the subsequent apologies and corrective actions were too late, an indication on how challenging it is for organizations to develop their communication applications during crises.

Social media networks have become strong magnifiers of reputational impact in the digital age. Viral controversies, criticisms, or negative sentiments can quickly spread across borders and reach various audiences around the world. The viral nature of social media multiplies the importance of timely and strategic responses to limit reputation damage.

Organizations that don't realize or do not want to use Social Media with a proactive approach will ultimately lose control of their narrative, potentially seriously hurting their reputation.

A clear example is the social media drama involving fashion brand H & M in 2018. There was a lot of uproar after an advertisement that was portrayed as offensive to many, a young black boy in a hoodie with the same phrase. The situation not only resulted in the demand for boycotting but also raised criticism involving cultural insensitivity. First, the reputational crisis is what H&M faced, highlighting the importance of anticipating and navigating cultural sensitivities in a globalized world where organizations have to work.

Proactive reputation management extends beyond the realm of crisis response, encompassing continuous initiatives to establish and reinforce positive perceptions. Organizations who pursue CSR, ethical business standards and community involvement accumulate a depository of goodwill which can also act as a beacon -shaped barrier during crises. Resilience in the case of reputation issues is increased by CSR measures not only because it brings well-being to society but also helps build public image.

In addition, organizational transparency has become a central pillar of successful reputation management. Ultimately, stakeholders include customers, investors and employees who appreciate the transparency of corporate behavior. In the information age where data is accessible for everyone, organizations that admit mistakes when they happen, are open to others and communicate in a transparent manner not only retain trust but also develop such culture.

139

Organizations that managed crises needed to consider how long reputational damage would last. While an unclean reputation may take some time to disappear, it can shape the choices of consumers; influence investor confidence and other facets such as stakeholder relationships for a relatively long period. Trust-building is usually a long and delicate process requiring consistent efforts to prove sincere intent of change for the better.

Regulatory Compliance Issues

The impacts of not following the laws go beyond just getting a fine and include reputational damage, which reduces an organization's credibility within its industry as well as with all stakeholders. Owing to dynamic aspects of regulatory terrain and mounting vigilance on ethics, it is also essential for organizations not only to fulfill current compliance standards but constantly adjust themselves with changing regulatory landscapes while overthrowing the highest ethical practices.

Any failure to abide by laws or regulations can breed a chain of legal and financial ramifications that have adverse effects on the survival capacity of an organization. Regulatory organizations, having the authority enshrined in their mandate to impose penalties on entities breaching compliance have powers of imposition for fines, sanctions and legal action.

The financial losses that may result from no conformance in this instance can be huge, undermining profitability, liquidity and other aspects of sustainable sources.

There are many cases, including antitrust violations and environmental transgressions where organizations were slapped with fines running into millions of dollars to underscore extensively the ramifications of failing to comply.

An example of this is the Volkswagen emission scandal that shed light on what happens when regulatory compliance fails. In 2015, it was uncovered that Volkswagen had used software in their diesel cars to cheat the emissions tests thereby violating environmental laws. The impact was significant fines, lawsuits and a legal blow that took the dignity out of Volkswagen. The case highlighted not only the financial consequences of failing to comply but also how even if legal battles are settled, lingering reputational damage can result.

The regulatory environment is a dynamic one and this creates an even bigger problem for most organizations as they strive to maintain compliance. The regulatory mechanisms adapt to the changing social landscape, emerging technologies and lessons from previous disasters. Organizations operating across jurisdictions come up against a multitude of regulations, all liable to changes and modifications.

The inability to adjust and keep up with these changes may lead to unintentional non-compliance like the case of General Data Protection Regulation (GDPR) that was introduced in the European Union. Many companies were rushing to get their data protection practices in line with the new laws, being penalized for non-compliance.

Ethical concerns entangled with regulatory compliance reinforce the imperative for organizations to settle upon ethical behavior as an essential aspect of their running principle. When illegal practices are frequent even when they do not violate the existing regulations, companies can suffer reputational crises and lose stakeholders' trust.

The after-effects of corruption in a business, as it relates to fraudulent financial activities or dishonest marketing practices and discriminatory employment policies are not only limited by the law but they also influence an organization's social license.

The financial sector presents a suitable field in which the interaction between regulatory compliance and ethical concerns is apparent. Incidents of banks indulging in malpractices like Wells Fargo fake accounts scandal demonstrated the consequences for foregoing ethics to benefit from short-term gains.

Despite its efforts to settle the administrative violations, Wells Fargo had not only thousands of dollars in fines but also a humiliating reputation during years. It is an example that ethical misconduct usually has a lasting impact on stakeholder trust at any time.

As organizations are faced with the tricky landscape of regulatory compliance, technology is being used more and more to get results. Regulatory technology, or RegTech, is an area that evolves as a field whereby advanced analytics using AI and automation help in compliance management. These platforms enable organizations to cost-effectively process regulatory obligations, conduct compliance in real time and optimize reporting procedures.

The integration of RegTech does not only improve operational efficiency but also places organizations in a favorable position to move around the intricate complexities that come with evolving regulatory landscapes fast and effectively.

Further, a strong compliance culture in organizations is essential to promote proactive behavior towards compliance. This entails cultivating a culture of responsibility and sensitizing employees at all levels on the necessity for compliance in their day to day activities. A compliance culture, however, is much more than just a checklist—it involves instilling ethical ethos into the organization's very DNA; creating an environment where law and regulation

144

adherence becomes collective responsibility other than as mere regulatory obligations.

The importance of corporate governance structures in promoting compliance with regulation cannot be overemphasized. Directors board, audit committee and internal control systems have key roles in the oversight function as well as risk assessment compliant monitoring. However, their efficiency depends upon the autonomy of such governance structures and how they realize themselves as a bulwark against compliance failures.

Global Supply Chain Disruptions

The global supply chain disruptions remain one of the most serious threats to organizations, revealing weaknesses that could lead to catastrophic results. The interdependencies among these supply chains, as they promote efficiency and cost-benefit relationships between individual businesses, equally imperil those same companies because of geopolitical tensions or from trade wars; health pandemics generate the plight. The consequences of these interruptions are far-reaching, not only affecting the immediate manufacturing processes but also organization resilience and sustainability at large.

Interdependencies of the global economy are amongst critical factors contributing to this crisis. Companies, trying to cut costs and improve efficiency, create complicated global intertwined supply networks across nations and continents. Although this globalization strategy provides benefits, it also creates vulnerability to market shocks. Tensions of geopolitical nature, which include trade wars and diplomatic standoffs quickly turn into hindrances towards smooth flow of goods and services.

The volatility of global politics is one area where trade disputes, which are a recurring theme and can cascade into problems for supply chains. Tariffs, trade barriers, and retaliatory measures create disruptions in existing trade circuits that cause delays and increased costs as well a recalibration of sourcing practices. For businesses that depend heavily on certain markets, these disruptions can be fiscally devastating and harm profitability as well.

Health emergencies like the global pandemic of recent years highlight the vulnerability of international supply chains. Lockdowns, restrictions on movement and labor shortages can spiral from an outbreak of infectious diseases. But not only do these factors disrupt production but they also reveal the danger of relying on particular regions for manufacturing and inputs. Such supply chain bottlenecks in the following have an echo effect on various industries such as technology, health care and auto.

In addition, reliance on a sole provider of critical components or materials complicates the challenges associated with supply chain disruptions. Organizations usually practice single-sourcing to ease their operations and bargain with suppliers in order to achieve the best deal. Still, this approach puts them at risk of disturbances from the supply side; whether it comes as a result of natural disasters or political unrest or anything else that was not predicted. Diversification of suppliers is required to reduce such risks and a more sustainable supply chain.

Lack of risk assessment only makes disruptions worse. In pursuit of short-term gains, many organizations may ignore holistic risk evaluation strategies. However, their inability to predict and prepare for uncertainty leaves companies unprepared when problems arise. Robust risk management is characterized by scenario planning, supply chain mapping and ongoing monitoring to detect existing vulnerabilities that can be addressed through the development of mitigation strategies.

Supply chain disruption has deep financial repercussions. Among the operational costs are high lead times, costly transportation fees and alternative sourcing. Stockouts and delays in fulfilling customer orders can also cost a company revenue and damage its reputation. Summing up, cumulative impact may result in the reduced shareholder value and market competency.

In addition, supply chain disruptions can create problems with customer relationships and undermine trust. Dissatisfied clients, late deliveries and product shortages can result in loss of long-term customers. While effective crisis management is indeed necessary to rebuild trust and regain customer confidence, preventive measures that focus on keeping future interruptions at bay are just as critical.

Environmental and Sustainability Issues

Environmental and sustainability challenges form an impeding source of crises for organizations under the purview far beyond operational disruptions which entail reputational threats to organizations as well as existence.

With this age of greater attention to climate change, ecological degradation and changing societal needs businesses find themselves in a complicated world where environmental mistakes can run far reaching implications. Failure of sustainable practices, climate-related events and environmental disasters not only threaten social license to operate but poses real risks for companies' long term viability.

Climate-related events are one of the main points on the spectrum of the environmental crisis. The rising occurrence and magnitude of events like hurricanes, floods, wildfires and abnormal weather developments reveal that the effects of climate change are deeply felt. Companies operating in areas susceptive to such events are at an increased risk of supply chain, infrastructure disruptions and business continuity.

Despite the fact that climate-related disasters often lead to a great deal of recovery work, serious material losses and also most importantly reputational damage.

Man-made environmental disasters ranging from industrial accidents, oil spillages or other such events present organizations with critical dangers. Besides the short-term environmental disaster, such accidents instigate a chain of events. Liabilities, regulation inquiries and clean up costs increase fast affecting the financial condition.

In addition, the reputational damage is likely to linger for many years pulling down stakeholder confidence and investor sentiment. The disastrous Deepwater Horizon oil spill remains a moving example of how an environmental tragedy can have catastrophic effects on the reputation and performance of a company.

Sustainability issues such as depletion of resources, pollution and social injustice are crucial aspects adorning the landscape of the environmental crisis. The current age of heightened consciousness and in regard to corporate social responsibility dictates change in organizations' practices begging on some sustainable principles. A failure to show a reasonable amount of commitment towards sustainable business practices not only puts companies at regulatory and legal accountability but also deters environmentally-friendly consumers and investors.

In the environmental and sustainability paradigm, meeting social needs is a complex challenge to organizations. Both consumers and those who invest in companies are becoming more critical of such entities not only concerning the improved economic performance but also regarding environmental sustainability and social responsibility. Failure to adapt to changing norms and avoid crooked behavior, which will thoroughly deplete brand value distinction in the market.

On the contrary, firms that take a proactive approach to embracing sustainability as part of their core business philosophy can boost brand image while attracting customers who are more concerned about social responsibility and reduce risks related with changing societal values.

Environmental and sustainability lapses are some of the most elusive threats that a firm can receive. During a world of instant communication and increased public attention, the news about environmental neglect or unsustainable activities can be quickly revealed which magnified reputational loss. Social media acts as a megaphone, transmitting both positive and negative news; therefore it is apparently vital for an enterprise to watch over its ecological footprint and sustainability practices.

Operational crises resulting from environmental factors come out in various ways. Sustainability craze in the world leads to many regulatory interventions that can be rather mandatory for companies. Non-compliance not only results in monetary fines but also physical business interruptions. Also, resource scarcity or environmental regulations or customer preferences for sustainable sourcing may disrupt supply chains leading to production problems and the profitability.

For addressing the intricacies in environmental and sustainability problems, it is essential for organizations to develop proactive integrated frameworks. This requires not only adherence to current environmental regulations but also the ability to forecast emerging regulatory trends.

However, developing sustainable practices is an integral part of building resilience which includes circular economy principles, lowering carbon footprints and investing in renewable sources.

Further, developing a climate of openness and responsibility is essential. Frequent updates regarding environmental impact, sustainability programs, and other milestones not only helps to foster trust with stakeholders but also proves the company is invested in perceptual development. Industry cooperation with competing entities, NGOs and government agencies can lead to the establishment of industry standards and best practices.

Failure to Innovate

The lack of innovation looms large over institutions as an omen to crisis for those who refuse to keep up with technology advancements and changes in market trends or consumer behavior. In an age characterized by fast innovation and shattering innovations, such stagnation means that the organizations quickly become obsolete as they are not adapted to their volatile market environments. This inertia, however, has far-reaching implications about a firm's identity and ability to address rapidly changing challenges of the business environment.

Technological advances serve as a critical agent of change, propelling sectors ahead and transforming the competitive market. Companies that do not take advantage of the emerging technologies will lag behind in both operational efficiency and product quality.

The introduction of artificial intelligence, Blockchain and the Internet of Things brings with it a wave of transformational opportunities ranging from more efficient business processes to new models entirely. If these technologies are not integrated into operations, organizations become exposed to competition that uses innovation as a strategic advantage.

Market changes, as a consequence of altering behaviors among the consumers, world economy trends or geopolitical situations pose very great challenges to organizations. Failure to predict deviations from these directions may lead to a mismatch between company's supply and market requirements.

Kodak's failure to quickly adapt to the emerging digital photography revolution exemplifies that a misjudgment of such changes can lead straight down into a plunge. The ability to decode market signals, predict trends and respond with rapid strategic repositioning of the business is critical for organizational hold.

Consumer preferences are affected by various changes like societal values and emerging lifestyle trends from a dynamic force that shapes the industries. Organizations that fail to take the changing nature of consumer expectations seriously risk losing their audience. Sustainability consciousness, for instance, has forced companies to reassess products packaging and even corporate culture. By failing to keep pace with shifting consumer preferences, organizations lose their relevance of the market and also risk damaging their reputation and edge out customers.

The effects of the inability to innovate are more far reaching than mere financial losses. One of the negative effects that arise as a result of stagnation is loss in attractiveness to quality personnel because innovative professionals seek organizational environments conducive for innovation and continuous improvement.

Failure to innovate can likewise result in operational inefficiencies that prevent the organization from maintaining agility and responsiveness when confronted with unanticipated events. The destruction of the competitive advantage is not an overnight phenomenon but a mere continuous slip that demands organizations to adopt innovation proactively.

Cultural, structural or managerial resistance to change is a strong obstacle for innovation. As "we have always done it this way" becomes a precursor for an upcoming crisis in the organizations which are unwilling to adopt change. The case of the Blockbuster-Netflix saga is used as a warning – if only the former had embraced digital streaming, Netflix would not have turned its industry upside down. Organizations need to nurture a culture that encourages experimentation, appreciates agility and sees change as an opportunity rather than threat.

The consequences of an inability to innovate are felt throughout the organizational environment. The innovation culture is greatly determined by leadership. Advocates who promote continuous learning, dedicate funds to R&D initiatives, and shape a future-oriented attitude propel innovation. On the other hand, leadership that continues to hold on to old paradigms or rejects needed transformations can be the pinch point blocking innovation from developing roots.

Collaboration, internal and external to the organization itself has played as a key catalyst for innovation. It is through the creation of cross-functional teams that can exploit diverse perspectives and skill sets that creative solutions necessarily are developed. In addition, associating with stakeholders from the external environment such as start ups, research institutions or industry disruptors is another best practice that often fosters innovation. An enterprise that establishes a collaborative relationships network can take advantage of external reserves and stay abreast of changing trends in the industry.

CHAPTER 4

A New Level of Leadership

Success is a shared theme that binds vast numbers of people together in their desires. It is a general desire, an echo in the hallways of dreams reverberating with hope for better and greater tomorrow. However, within this shared dreaming is only one bittersweet reality: the ever widening gap between wishing for success and being ready to withstand change on an individual scale.

Wishful thinking versus workable dedication is a recurring theme that often characterizes the difference between those who wish and those whose wishes materialize. Most harbor the deep desire for success, imagining themselves on top of their quests. But as they are faced with the difficult task of walking along this grueling and challenging path from the present moment to what they envision for their next level, a discernible hesitancy surfaces.

Think of the pattern, which leaders throughout history reached great heights. Transformational heroes like Nelson Mandela, Mahatma Gandhi or Steve Jobs didn't simply want to succeed; they took up what it required sacrifices and struggles that made them transform into great people. Mandela suffered years of captivity because of the principles he fought for, Gandhi struggled with nonviolent struggles and Jobs survived stormy waters in business.

And the core of their success was not only about wishes but steadfastness to go through challenges, fight with difficulties and change themselves as personalities and professionals. They knew that the journey to the next level does not transpire on wishful thinking; rather, it requires grit, sacrifice and perseverance even in spite of hardships.

A fear of the unknown is one of the main obstacles towards overcoming this gap, between aspirations and actualization. Going from a stable environment in the present to an unknown land of the above level is always disconcerting. It requires leaving one's comfort zone and facing uncertainties, accepting discomfort. But exactly in these uncomfortable spheres, the seeds of transformation are planted.

Additionally, the passage to a higher level requires adjustment of mindset. It includes replacing limiting beliefs with a mindset of growth. People who are tied to the limitations they imposed upon themselves find their roots in a circle of dreamers with no proper progress. What drives individuals to the next level is the boldness of questioning one's own beliefs, combined with an unparalleled determination for improvement.

For it does not take one person to endure what is needed for moving from the present state into a higher level; often there has to be support groups. Building a network of mentors, allies and having a community around that also promotes growth becomes very important. Smart leaders appreciate the secret strength of teamwork and teachship, pooling knowledge to overcome obstacles in their race towards victory.

In the limitless horizon of wishes and progress towards higher ground, it is leadership that makes people move from wishful thinking to full realization. The difference between those who want to succeed and those that will end up getting there lies in being able not just to have the desires but be equipped with zeal and insight beyond one's own present vision of horizon.

The ability to think beyond what is common among people does not characterize passive dreamers like proactive leaders. Their vision serves as a compass which guides them through the process of change. Having an eye for challenges in advance, it is this proactive attitude of such people that enables them to come up with innovative strategies and go through the uneven pathway between here and now.

Moreover, great leaders have a source of motivation that is driven by their steadfast vision. Such a desire becomes not only their goal but also the driving force that pushes them on even when walking seems to be challenging. The motivation to achieve success and a clearly defined vision becomes the powerful agent that makes them tough enough to survive all trials during their journey towards greatness.

It is not just in the success of personal actions, but rather by enhancing those around them that effective leadership consists. Broader thinking allows leaders to create an atmosphere in which the personal purposes, shared by all members of a team equally contribute towards common goals. They create a chain of followers who are compelled to share the vision and thus rise above their individual wishes towards one next level.

Additionally, through their visionary powers proactive and innovative leaders are enabled to peer into the future before it manifests. It is a special skill that makes them the leaders in change, builders of fate. Through foresight, timeliness, and gracefully navigating the unmapped waters, these leaders guide a course that others might not even have seen.

We are not able to rectify our large problems if we try to use the same kind of logic that rendered them. Most people are good, and few want to make the effort of going from being good to achieving greatness; and that's what our next generation leadership is all about. For your firm to scale up, the new heights that you are trying to achieve can't just be in your head. You must act, and it will require some severe toil.

Feel the Emotion of the Future Before it Happens

Visualization and experiencing emotionally the envisioned results indicate that you feel the emotion of your future before it occurs. It can be put into practice by leaders to develop a positive and forward-looking mentality, improving the capacity of making strategic decisions. Leaders who imaginatively connect to envisioned success can emanate enthusiasm, resilience and tenacity – processes which change intentions towards actions of the leaders themselves as well as inspiring those they lead.

Linking emotionally with the future helps leaders be aware of potential threats, because it makes them objects to emotions. This transcends conventional risk assessments by utilizing instinct and foresight. The more leaders are capable of empathetically internalizing the emotions that different crisis scenarios evoke, the better they can pick up early warning signs and anticipate unfolding events.

This preventative strategy allows proactive crisis planning and the building of resources, plans, strategies as well as contingency plans before a pending situation becomes imminent.

Positive emotions implied in imagining overcoming crises play a role of contributing to mental resilience for leaders. This resilience serves as a mental armor that allows leaders to possess a clear and focused state of mind during chaos. Through internalizing success scenarios, leaders can develop a mindset based on the belief that challenges are growth opportunities and not insurmountable obstacles. This mental toughness acts as a driving force, allowing leaders to navigate through critical times with confidence and clarity.

A leader's emotional involvement in future scenarios boosted strategy decisions during a crisis.

Emotional leaders are able to visualize the impact a decision may cause on an organization and its shareholders based on how they feel associated with success. This emotional intuition enables leaders to make decisions more confidently; they find strategies that correspond with ideals, mission and long-term ambitions.

Strategy becomes a collaborative thing with strong emotional connection to the future desired state.

In the midst of crises, leaders who emotionally connect to positive outcomes are effective in motivating and inspiring their teams. By providing a captivating picture of achievement, leaders inspire people's sense of purpose and commitment. This emotional affiliation forges a unified and enthusiastic workforce, allowing the team to share a collective belief that obstacles can be overcome.

The leader's capacity to transmit the pleasant feeling of success becomes a much needed tool in sustaining morale, promoting team spirit and persistence under sufferings.

Crisis management requires emotional resonance in the way we communicate. Managers who genuinely experience the emotions related to positive results can appear genuine and loving in their messages. This emotional bond creates a channel to convey the message of hope and confidence during turbulent times; hence, making team members more likely to trust another leader.

With a humanized message that cuts through emotional barriers, clear communications become the stabilizing element behind an organization during times of turbulence and uncertainty.

Fostering the emotion of the future promotes an attitude to change and progress in a group. Leaders who are psychologically committed to positive outcomes motivate members of the team to work creatively and collaboratively.

This leads to that change becoming so embraced that challenges are seen as opportunities for innovation and new solutions need to be experimented. The team members, guided by the positive emotional aura of an effective leader covet flexibility in their adoption to changes with better willingness to try innovative approaches towards problem solving.

The leaders who experience the feeling of the future contribute immensely towards creating a positive organizational culture, especially during crises. The tone of the organization is set by the leaders' emotional resilience and optimism. Seeing their leaders' positive emotional connection with success, the members of a team are more likely to develop this kind of attitude.

This common positive attitude becomes a cultural basis laying the ground for mutual cooperation, supportiveness and shared conviction that even obstacles can be met successfully. Alternatively, positive organizational culture fosters higher resilience and agility as well as the ability to face crises with a common front.

Feeling the emotion of the future is shared with learning from positive and negative emotional activities. Reflecting on past crises, leaders can see the emotional angles of their own decision-making and what happened next. This self-reflective process improves a leader's consciousness, enabling them to understand how their emotions affect leadership and decision in crisis periods. The lessons from emotional experiences become an ongoing cycle of continuous improvement, yielding valuable information that leaders can use to enhance their crisis management capabilities and modify approaches for future difficulties.

Emotional preparedness brings confidence to leaders and team members during challenging times. Leaders who genuinely feel the emotions accompanying positive results exude confidence and self-affirmation. This confidence becomes infectious, causing it to spread throughout the team. When team members see their leaders emotionally engaged in a vision of success, they will be more inclined in trusting the leadership ability to guide through a crisis.

This trust underlies a strong team that can respond to adversity knowing there is shared understanding and confidence in the guidance of leadership.

The sensation of feeling the emotion allows leaders to think in terms of long-term perspectives during crises. Instead of responding to short-term pressures, leaders who are emotionally connected with the positive outcomes continue and remain focused on broadening 'the big picture' targets.

This value agreement with long-term goals directs decision making by following through that the decisions made during a crisis are sketched in line with where the organization is headed. A long-term point of view is a stabilizing factor that allows leaders and teams to act in the present but maintain their focus on what lies ahead.

How You View Situations is How You Tackle Them

The connection between a crisis leader's perception and action are also central to good leadership. Leaders who treat challenges not as insurmountable barriers but just opportunities are more likely to approach crisis with a proactive and constructive problem-solving attitude. This view allows them to look for creative solutions, work with their teammates, and learn from the lessons that they need improvement.

However, an individual with a negative or reactive stance may be reluctant to take the necessary steps in times of crisis as they procrastinate and act defensively. This responsive approach may prevent the leader from managing difficulties appropriately, slowing down their responses and worsening a crisis's consequences.

The approach to problem-solving by a crisis leader is directly influenced by their ability to analyze situations proactively. Proactive individuals would instead approach problem solving in advance so as to prevent issues from escalating into a complete crisis. Such a proactive approach includes risk assessment, scenario planning and prevention measures.

By adopting this approach to challenges, leaders can use the organization's early symptoms as strategic opportunities that will allow them to solve problems before they become full-blown crises and lead a crisis response team in an orderly manner. This differs from reactive leaders, who act when problems crop up and often result in firefighting with inefficient crisis management.

Nevertheless, the crisis leader's point of view plays a crucial role in deciding to act on days and moments challenging. Leaders who think strategically assess the long-term implications of their decisions so that they can ensure alignment with broader goals and values in an organization. Through this strategic alignment crisis responses promote general organizational resilience and adaptability.

On the other hand, leaders who do not think in a strategic way may make decisions based on immediate issues without any regard to long-term goals weighed against short-lived profits.

The strategic capacity to perceive challenges leads the leaders to the expectation that organizations should be led through crises with foresight and zeal for sustained success.

An attitude that sees challenges as opportunities for innovation and adaptation serves as a drive behind organizational development during times of crisis. Innovation-oriented leaders approach challenges with an innovative perception, motivating their teams to engage in new solutions. In this outlook, crises are also seen as windows of opportunity:

moments to reassess processes; embrace the change and strengthen resilience.

On the other hand, leaders who view challenges as merely problems to be solved will miss opportunities for innovation and never capitalize on what is possible. One of the key characteristics that make effective crisis leaders is their ability to instill an innovative and adaptable mindset, which shapes how organizations change in periods after crises.

The approach of a crisis leader significantly influences the formation of organizational culture, particularly in difficult times. Leaders who uphold a positive attitude even at the time of crisis generate confidence and optimism among their followers. This overall sense of positivity is contagious, encouraging team members to tackle challenges from a positive standpoint.

A culture of collaboration, mutual support, and a conviction that challenges can be overcome is fostered by the capacity for hope demonstration among leaders. Alternatively, leaders who have a pessimistic or defeatist view may unknowingly encourage a climate of fear, demotivation and anxiety. What an individual perceives as the organizational culture has a crucial impact on how teams work together, create breakthroughs and endure in crisis.

The emotional intelligence of the crisis leader deeply determines how a man views situations, and this is what defines his actions. Leaders with high levels of emotional intelligence are able to identify and control their own emotions as well as others. This emotional sensibility allows leaders to navigate crises with compassion, clarity and clear messages. The perception of the leader informed by emotional intelligence affects connection with team members emotionally based on trust and synchronization.

On the other hand, emotionally insensitive leaders may not identify with their team's emotions and this is likely to result in communication barriers stumping morale as well as an unsuccessful crisis response. The skills of emotional intelligence give a leader the tools to see every challenge through an empathetic lens, thus enabling him or her to lead with compassion and get their team out on the other side of turmoil.

A strategic mindset of a crisis leader can be displayed through maintaining the long- term vision while facing crises. Synoptically focusing on the vision and mission of an organization, leaders may take decisions in accordance with its strategic direction. This long-term vision provides the commitment that crisis responses have led to sustained success through difficulties.

The leaders who emphasize a long-term vision look at the lasting consequences of their choices, resulting in an organizational culture focused on resiliency and flexibility. On the contrary, leaders who consider only short-term gains can make decisions that destroy long-term goals and compromise future success of an organization. Effective leaders demonstrate the ability to sustain a 'vision of things five years hence' in times of crisis, which shapes and defines future trajectories and resilience capabilities.

Building Leadership Team for Crisis

A company has a crisis, and its top management cannot communicate well or make decisions properly. One of the problems is that this overcritical and micromanaging CEO creates tension and resentment in his team. At the same time, the CFO is focusing on financials saying 'no' to any change that may affect its performance. Surrounded by these conflicting demands, the COO has a conflict between what the CEO and CFO demand on him while also supporting his team.

Being under enormous pressure, the team makes a lot of mistakes and the rising anger of the CEO does not help to relieve them. The CFO, who is worried about the cost of such mistakes, wants increased vigor to correct them. The confused COO is not able to maneuver through the crisis.

The issue that needs to be addressed is clear—the leadership team doesn't work together as a unit. Mistakes, conflict and a negative work environment result from poor communication, conflicting priorities and lack of support. Change is inevitable for team success.

First, the leadership team needs to admit that there is a problem. The CEO must focus on their leadership approach, taking into account its consequences for the team and deciding to change it. The CFO should also widen sights beyond the bottom line to take into account that a company is more than its immediate profitability. The COO should fight for the team and request changes that would make talking and working together better.

The second is the planning for change. Goals, planning the timeline and ways of measurement are essential. Tracking conflicts, errors, and employee satisfaction can help measure success.

The implementation of the plan requires commitment and persistence. Regular monitoring to evaluate progress and make any required changes is crucial. This continual process requires the team's dedication for sustainable change.

For a leader to build a very strong team for a crisis and the overall performance of the organization, the following strategies must be adopted.

Identify Core Competencies

A thoughtful analysis of the key skills and characteristics necessary for crisis control is required to construct a leadership team that can take into account crises. The first step is considered the strategic base of an entire crisis leadership edifice.

Basically, core competencies refer to the basic skills and attributes that leaders need in order not just survive but thrive when crisis strikes. Such competencies extend beyond the common attributes of leadership and focus on those capabilities needed in managing during a crisis.

But decisiveness is the most important competency. Leadership needs to demonstrate agile decision-making capabilities in uncertainty. Leaders in a crisis must be able to assess situations quickly and act decisively, aligned with an organization's mission and codes of conduct.

Adaptability is another critical competency. The landscape of the crisis fluid dynamics is always changing. Leaders should be adaptive, responding to change by adapting strategies and being persistent in the face of challenges. A leader that is adaptive can guide the team through unexpected situations, displaying a capability of learning and adjustments where required.

Clear communication skills are indispensable. Therefore, leaders should share their vision clearly as well as decisions and expectations; the flow of information needs to be smooth within a team and beyond. During such problems, communication is the hinge that kills misunderstandings and aligns actions ensuring understanding on all sides.

Leaders navigate the storm with a compass of strategic thinking. It is a predictive kind of approach that takes into account both immediate demands and long-term repercussions. Leaders need to be able to develop and implement such plans that will not only take care of immediate needs but also prepare the organization for its revival along with further development.

179

Collaboration is a competency that becomes all the more critical in crisis leadership. It is vital to be able to promote collaboration, multiple points of views and foster an atmosphere where group intelligence reaches its potential. While a group of people that works as one team can address tough issues better than any isolated individuals, cooperation is beneficial when it comes to solving problems.

Although these competencies offer a broad foundation, it is also essential to adjust some of them to the unique circumstances and profile characterizing an organization. Different crises require different capabilities, and leaders must be sensitive to the intricacies of their environment.

Pragmatically, the core competence identification process requires a detailed analysis of an organization's objectives , possible crisis events and the complexities involved in combating them. This evaluation has to include the response of major stakeholders, including current team members since it should consider all aspects that make this organization specific.

In addition, comparing industry best practices or drawing lessons from past crises whether inside the organization itself or external could help sharpen competence identification. Learning from success and failure allows us to perceive what skills are more valuable in the furnace of adversity.

Access Current Team Members

Evaluating the current team members is also an important part of efficient leadership as well as organizational development. To thoroughly assess current team members, it is critical to use a structured approach that takes into account identified competencies and therefore determines both weaknesses and strengths of the team.

To begin this assessment, it is crucial to precisely specify the competencies that are relevant for these objectives within a team and which reflect such a mission of an organization itself. These skills could range from specialized expertise to communication savvy, flexibility, problem-solving capabilities and team collaboration. Creating a strong structure of competencies will help leaders develop an objective system for assessing team members.

Employment of this assessment is practical when there are diverse tools and methods used. Conventional methods of collecting insights on individual team members include surveys, interviews as well as performance reviews. Surveys may include self-evaluation in addition to evaluations from peers and supervisors, providing a comprehensive perspective on each member of the team's strengths and weaknesses. Structured interviews enable engaging discourses which generate qualitative data to complement quantitative evaluations.

First, formal assessments of employees are not the only way to learn more about teams. Leaders should note closely the ways in which team members participate in projects, communicate with peers and respond to challenges. Such observations offer the practical approach to competency identification that is not clear from formal evaluation only.

Identifying team competencies' gaps entails identifying the places where individual members do not reach standards. This may be anything from lack of technical skills to issues posed in interpersonal communication and problem solving. There is no intent to pinpoint fault here, but rather where the targeted development efforts can improve overall team effectiveness.

On the other hand, it is just as important to identify strengths within your team. Recognizing and using existing strengths can enhance the performance of a team member and make it more pleasant for them to work. Points about the strengths of team members can also be specified to boost morale and motivation, establishing a sense of value as well as achievement.

Finally, after the assessment is over, strategies to mitigate gaps and leverage strengths are formulated. This may include specific training programs, mentor projects or rearrangement of team responsibilities according to respective skills. The objective is to establish a vibrant setting where team members are ever-changing into meeting the needs of an organization.

Recruitment and Selection

Recruitment and selection are core functions in creating a high-performance team, which requires an appropriate strategy to get the right people. In this engagement, we look at the practical considerations of hiring external candidates who possess diverse views and crisis management skills.

While recruiting external candidates, it is important that the recruitment strategy should be in sync with the organization's goals and values. The need for the external talent should be established on a solid knowledge about current team representation, skill sets and opportunities of gaps. This understanding provides a basis for developing job profiles that properly describe the necessary competencies, including those with crisis management skills.

In order to promote diversity, recruitment should not be limited by traditional sources. Utilizing several platforms such as the niche job boards, professional networks and industry specific events it is possible to widen the candidates' pool. In addition, collaborations with organizations dedicated to diversity can help in the recruitment of minority candidates promoting a more diverse workforce.

When selecting candidates, attention should be paid to evaluating them for both technical skills and culture. Structured interviews, competency-based tests and scenario based exercises can shed light on the candidate's crisis management skills. In real life situations and behavioral questions, candidates can reveal their skills to deal with difficult or complex problems.

In the search for various viewpoints, one ought to think not only about demographic diversity but also cognitive variety and wideness of perception. This entails seeing past superficial qualities and exploring a candidate's distinctive professional journey, accomplishments, and problem-solving methods. Diversity brings in more ideas and potential solutions, an area of particular interest during situations where creative thinking is usually necessary.

The other realistic aspect of that is conducting in-depth reference checks. It also means that recruiters would contact previous employers,

185

colleagues or mentors to get insights into a candidate's crisis management skills and overall work performance. This is the key step in determining if claims made during an interview are true and to ascertain that the selected candidate actually has required skills.

In addition, using an interview setting that includes a panel format with different types of interviewers would allow for a holistic assessment. Several perspectives lead to a comprehensive appreciation of the candidate's appropriateness and fit into an organization and team. This method also reflects the intention to create an environment in which diversity of opinions is appreciated.

However successful external candidates are, onboarding becomes a critical part of the process. A coherent onboarding process guarantees that newcomers adapt well to the culture of an organization and understand their role in crisis management. This entails availing relevant training, resources and mentorship to ease their incorporation into the team.

Define Roles and Responsibilities

The basis for good teamwork and appropriate strategic response in the realm of crisis management resides on well-defined roles and responsibilities that are distributed between each member. This precise demarcation not only promotes organizational unity but also takes advantage of individual strengths, which becomes essential during periods of crisis.

In the following analysis, we will carefully explore how roles and responsibilities can be constructed to not only suit individual team members' strengths but also complement crisis management strategy.

First, it is important to note that crises are ever-changing and include both natural disasters such as hurricanes or floods and computer and data breaches. This variability highlights the need for an adaptable team arrangement because each crisis requires a different reaction.

Thus, the first stage of role definition requires a comprehensive study of the area in which many crisis scenarios can be identified and their corresponding challenges. This vision facilitates the development of flexible roles and makes sure that team members can be agile in responding to changing situations.

In the shadow of a crisis, individual team members' strengths and competencies become central. This requires a careful analysis of the skills, experience and capabilities. Such roles allow not only increasing the overall team efficiency but also improving personal level of self-confidence. For example, a colleague specializing in communication and public relations may be very good at the position of spokesperson providing correct and relevant information to stakeholders.

Along with skill congruence, critical attention to personality characteristics and work styles is essential. Crisis management team is a microcosm of various talents and blending these unique characters creates some sort of uniformity in the unit. However, an introverted team member may thrive in technical settings where meticulous research is required or detailed plans have to be prepared while extroverts perform better as leaders and communicate effectively.

However, role definition requires a sophisticated analysis of the crisis management strategy. Thus, the roles should not work in isolation but instead form a coherent picture contributing to an overarching strategy. This requires transparency upon the team, in order for members to understand how their roles form part of a bigger picture. Additional training sessions and simulations can further improve these roles, preparing the team to be able to handle such crisis situations effectively.

In the implementation of roles and responsibilities, flexibility is sought as a prerequisite for success. Responses to crises are unpredictable and rooting for rigid on role definitions may be counterproductive. Hence, roles must be endowed with flexibility so that team members can work together efficiently and respond quickly to the arising challenges. This flexibility is not only an indication of the team's ability to overcome challenges but also a preemptive mechanism in addressing unexpected complications that form part of crisis management.

Do your team members perform the right functions? Others are doing more harm than good to the cause.

Create and develop an authentic leadership team. Select a type of leadership style that your business or organization can use. A real leadership type is one where you become an advocate of more ideas. Dictatorships never allow development because one person will make all the decisions and solve so many problems.

You need to bear in mind that a long-lasting, prosperous organization living after you cannot be attached if your organization is designed not to hold together past the moment of your departure. You ought to aim at the set target. This is a necessary component of the true leadership style and cannot be done in isolation. A powerful group who perform well in their respective domains with a properly laid out plan being clearly communicated is what you require.

If your business or organization is failing to progress, whether it comes from within and outside the company then you as a leader are the source of solutions. This vision should be basic and easy to understand. Therefore, major firms are not developing as they have relatively complicated structures, no adequate communication and team members do not fit into their areas of specialization.

Such organizations have complicated procedures, from decision-making to production and delivery. It is a big issue that every real leader should address.

One of the priorities that a true leader should ask himself or herself is: Did you document how everything has to be done in your organization? Are the people you work with aware of what processes and procedures they are undertaking? Are they assigned and placed according to their roles? Do they all perform the necessary procedures uniformly? Are they on track?

All these procedures are your responsibilities as a leader. You should be ready to work at your peak performance. This will necessitate you to polish your leadership qualities and work to the best of your abilities.

Communication and Collaboration

When I was young, I listened to older people because I was told you gain wisdom from them. This made me a good listener, a crucial foundation for effective communication. Listening helped me analyze situations and plan the next steps to solve them.

One day in school, one of my teachers had a very serious accident. A doctor's report indicated that he will have difficulty in hearing. This teacher had always emphasized on the need for his students to excel well through listening.

The whole class was quiet and confused about how listening could lead to effective communication. Though our teacher didn't explain, only urged us to practice, I wondered why some people inspire and motivate through effective speaking while others lack it.

Throughout my listening journey, I noticed many older people lacked this communication skill. Some raised poorly behaved children as they didn't provide parental advice. These children, growing up, had to break the cycle and educate themselves on life matters, a saddening experience for me.

One day, I told my teacher in front of the class that I'd been working on his assignment. I understood his emphasis on being good listeners for effective communication. I found two types of people in my work: those who can communicate effectively and those who lack the skill. In life, attracting and leading people is easiest through effective communication, a skill many leaders lack.

You've likely attended school, earned degrees and certificates. How did you manage that? By spending years in classes and seminars. How could you receive information if not communicated by lecturers or seminar hosts?

For many leaders, communication is a significant problem. The lack of it means no clear purpose for your team. Through communication, your team understands goals, future plans, etc., working together for a common purpose in your business or organization.

The first step is building the right team, but the emphasis after that will be fine-tuning needed skills. Communication and collaboration, often overlooked, play key roles. These skill-building programs become necessary. These programs should put an accent on the fact that communication is not only telling but making it effective to ensure appropriate timely information exchange by team members.

Additionally, such training programs need to inculcate some interactive exercises that promote an environment where teammates listen actively and articulate ideas collectively. By highlighting various communication styles and acknowledging cultural dimensions, the collaborative process can be made more inclusive and efficient.

Moreover, the introduction of up-to -date collaboration tools and platforms within training provides a team with necessary technological skills required for an effortless virtual cooperation reflecting the changing nature of working resources.

Building Trust and Cohesion

From the perspective of many people, trust is an intangible quality that defines a leadership team and lays as a foundation for true collaboration. To produce complex dynamics of organizational actions, creating an environment for openness and trust surpasses that of just jocularities because it entails a strategic need to make people work as reliable teams especially in uncertain times such as crisis.

One can picture trust as the glue that holds together all relationships in a leadership team. This is reflected in the confidence team members have with regard to one another's abilities, decisions and intentions. Fostering this trust is achieved via the avenues of open communication, harmonized behavior according to organizational values and common goals. A leadership team lacking trust loses its subtlety, making it difficult to cope with the trials of a crisis.

However, the formation of trust is not a passive process rather an active and conscious practice. The trust within the team is greatly influenced by

195

leaders. They have to create an atmosphere in which participants do not only feel authorized but motivated and even dare confess errors without the threat of penalty looming behind their shoulders. This culture of psychological safety enables people to contribute honestly, triggering a wave of creative and problem-solving power within the team.

Openness and trust are not just virtues but nothing more than strategies. When a group has to make decisions during the searing heat of a crisis and all doubts are obscure, if these people have faith in each other they can undertake unknown travels with ease. However, lack of trust can result in hesitation; questioning thence the partnership probably multiplying effects from the crisis.

The interdependence of trust and successful collaboration becomes even more obvious when the organization faces uncertainties associated with a disaster. In such decisive moments, the unity created through trust enables a team to act in unison and quick decision-making; changing tactics when need be as it is able to take on any opposition or challenge with ease. The concept of trust is no longer merely an element of culture but a competitive strength that pushes the team ahead despite difficult conditions.

Continuous Learning and Improvement

A strategic roadmap implicitly acknowledges the fluidity of challenges that arise from crises. In the strategic context, then continuous learning and improvement arise as guiding principles that nurture a culture of agility and adaptability to be critical for crisis leadership.

Crises are by their nature diffuse and random in occurrences. The tactics that work well today may face limitations in the light of increasing challenges tomorrow. Therefore, the focus on constant learning is not merely a positive attribute but an intentional necessity. This dedication to continuous learning not only covers personal skills but the group wisdom of all leadership members as well.

As a key element of continuous learning, the periodic revision and re-assessment of crisis response plans constitute an important aspect. The plans, which resemble living documents, should adjust accordingly to the changing nature of crises. Repeated assessments, informed by data from simulations, actual performances and industry benchmarks help the leadership team pinpoint improvement areas to change strategies ahead of time.

Normalizing continuous improvement within the team establishes a culture of adaptability. The members of the team learn that learning is not a single occurrence, but an ongoing process. This change of mindset enables the team to respond well and appropriately against these dynamic challenges posed by a crisis. It develops team resilience by iteration and refinement of its approaches to ensure that each experience contributes positively to overall crisis management capacity.

In addition, continuous learning provides a preventive action towards perceived risks. Through tracking emerging trends, technological breakthroughs and international developments the leadership team becomes an innovative organization that does not only respond to crises but foresaw them in advance. This premonition becomes a powerful tool that gives the team an advantage in traversing dynamic crises terrain.

They extend beyond skills related specifically to crisis. It involves leadership development as a whole. As the engine of the team, leaders must continuously develop leadership skills. This dual strategy combines crisis-specific skills into general leadership development in such a way that the team remains not only effective during crises but also possess tools for long term resilience to these.

Leadership and Coercion

This involves using force to effect change, persuading others into acting in a way that they do not want to and possibly tampering with rewards or penalties at their places of work.

The main difference is in the fact that coercive style does not represent an ideal model for leadership. In case of a vital threat that needs an immediate solution, other leaders may use coercion. This method involves applying pressure to yield results faster.

In this model, leaders are powerful and authority is centralized so most decisions are made with little or no input from team members. This is a command-type of approach in which the leader's commands are followed with little discussion. Although this approach works in some instances, it may restrict creativity and reduce employee involvement because there is no partaking of decision-making.

Leadership coercion that employs compulsion or force to control a team presents its own set of serious limitations, which can reduce both individual and collective performance within an organization.

Coercion may lead to an atmosphere of fear and tension in the teammates. For when leaders utilize threats or punishment, employees would be hesitant in sharing their ideas and initiating actions. The culture of fear would lead to timidity among individuals and could prevent them from expressing their views or suggesting alternative solutions for the image that they might be punished.

Coercion usually destroys the trust among a team. Trust is a foundation of a healthy workplace, and coercive leadership destroys this necessary attribute. However, coerced employees see their leaders as authoritarian figures and not mentors. This lack of trust minimizes teamwork because members tend to be reluctant in sharing information or working towards shared goals.

Another victim of coercion in leadership is employee morale. Constant pressure and fear of negative outcomes will result in low job satisfaction levels. However, when people are forced to work under pressure their motivation and zeal eventually diminishes which lowers overall productivity as well as the quality of what is being produced. Low morale can lead to increased rates of turnover since the employees look for a more positive and supportive work environment.

Additionally, coercion usually results in compliance more than commitment. People who are forced to obey orders may do so begrudgingly and without full commitment. This compliance-based approach does not succeed in creating an integrated team that is genuinely committed to the success of the organization. It is more likely to achieve sustainable success when people are fully motivated and dedicated in performing their duties.

Further, coercion suppresses free speech. Fearful culture negatively influences discussions between leaders and team members since the latter fear to communicate openly. To solve problems, share ideas and overcome challenges good communication is needed. Though coercive leadership encourages this vital component of teamwork, it creates obstacles in its way that impede the organization's efficacy.

The Role of Motivation

The notion of motivation as a factor that guides human behavior is rather complicated, while the difference between intrinsic and extrinsic motivation leads to success in leadership practices or personal development. These two types of motivation stand for different origins that form our behavior.

Intrinsic motivation arises from within, as people do an activity because of the pleasure or satisfaction it elicits. This motivation is by its nature tied to personal interests, passions and the enjoyment derived from doing the task. When people are intrinsically motivated, they enjoy the idea of engaging in something and feeling satisfied with their accomplishment instead of sticking to external rewards.

For example, there exists an employee that is intrinsically motivated who would want to undertake a challenging project not just for the sake of getting paid but because they are simply passionate about what they do and derive purpose from this. Intrinsic motivation is often linked to more creativity, innovation, and job enjoyment because people feel more closely connected with their work.

Alternatively, extrinsic motivation refers to rewards that are not connected with the behavior itself. This type of motivation is based on activities that lead to monetary benefits, reputation or praise. Although extrinsic motivation may help the accomplishment of quick goals and compliance, it will not be able to build-up long term commitment or develop real enthusiasm.

Imagine a student putting in the effort to study hard for a test just to get a good grade. The grade becomes like a prize for them. While this can make them do well in the short run, only relying on getting good grades might not make them truly love learning.

Good leaders know it's smart to mix both inside and outside motivations when working with a team. They get that getting people excited about the work itself is important. But sometimes, giving rewards for a job well done can be like a pat on the back. Finding this balance makes a workplace where team members aren't just working for rewards but also find joy in what they do.

Being a good leader means getting your team excited from the inside. Talk to them about the big picture, connect the vision to what they believe in. When people know their role matters, it gives them a special reason to work beyond just doing tasks.

Let your team have some freedom. People like feeling in control and making important choices. Give them chances to share ideas, take charge of projects, and be creative. This taps into what they naturally care about and makes them proud of their work.

Say 'good job' when it's deserved. Recognize and praise their hard work through words, awards, or just talking about their achievements in team meetings. Feeling seen and appreciated creates a strong connection to the work, making it personal and motivating.

Help your team grow. Offer chances for them to learn new things through mentorship or ongoing education. When people see they can get better at what they do, they naturally want to keep pushing themselves. It's like an internal motivation boost.

Create a supportive and friendly work environment. Encourage open communication, teamwork, and appreciation for different opinions. When your team feels like a family, it makes them want to do their best for the team's success.

Show your team the impact of their work. Share success stories, let them hear from happy customers, or show how their efforts make a real difference. Knowing they're making a positive impact keeps them motivated from the inside.

Conclusion

At the climax of this thorough investigation into crisis leadership, we reach the point where knowledge and action come together with theoretical grounds giving way for concrete practices. The undertaking, which unfolded from leadership principles definition to crisis recovery dynamics realization, has become a comprehensive guide for the managers operating in complex situations of turbulence.

Starting with a definition of leadership principles and the stages embedded in its multidimensional nature, we laid down strong foundations for understanding what governs effective leadership. This fundamental perception, focusing on identifying and evaluating crises in the framework of leadership, acts as a pillar upon which leaders can build their reactions to challenges.

The later chapters discussed the critical aspect of a crisis leader which revealed unique features that make for competent leadership in chaotic times. The focus went beyond on the decision-making point establishing leaders as builders of resilience in their organizations. The balance between authority and collaboration became one of the primary messages, pointing out how complex interplay is needed for effective crisis leadership.

Continuing in the wake of disasters, the guide adroitly traversed through recovery and reconstruction. This required a delicate approach of rebuilding trust in uncharted waters, designing tactics to win over and secure the support of stakeholders, and moving from immediate crisis containment to long-term recovery. Detailed long-term planning highlighted the enduring nature of successful leadership, ensuring its application even in the chronic period that followed earlier crisis management.

Integrating wisdom from historical and contemporary examples, the examination smoothly shifted to application-based insights. It empowers leaders to define their strategies according to the challenges that are presented by successful cases and failures in managing crises irrationally. The chapter on ethics in leadership revealed the process of upholding integrity and moral values amid crisis moments, giving practical advice for developing an ethical plan within a dynamic framework.

During the end of this journey, we have arrived in an epilogue that encourages leaders to look back on their long way through crisis leadership. This reflective lens serves as a poignant reminder that leadership is not an inalterable end-point but rather a transformation, one of continuous movement toward change and metamorphosis. The encouragement is apparent everywhere, reminding us that each challenge overcome becomes yet another chance to polish our reflections even further and apply the concepts we learned from reading this detail-packed guide.

Reader Reviews

I hope you're enjoying this book. Your feedback is invaluable to me and will guide me in creating even better content for future books.

Your review can inspire and guide others on their journey to financial freedom and personal growth. I believe that together, we can create a community of empowered individuals ready to transform their lives.
It will also help me adjust and improve on the subsequent books.

Your opinion matters, and I appreciate your support!

Scan this QR code to discover more about the author! Visit the Author Central page for exclusive insights and updates on more invaluable books

Thank You For Spending Your Time With Us